THE GOLDEN SWORD
STAMFORD RAFFLES
AND THE EAST

AUSPICIUM·MELIORIS·ÆVI

THE GOLDEN SWORD
STAMFORD RAFFLES
AND THE EAST

EDITED BY NIGEL BARLEY

Published for The Trustees of

The British Museum by

BRITISH MUSEUM PRESS

The Trustees of the British Museum acknowledge the generous support of

Standard ⚡ Chartered

This book is published to accompany an exhibition in the British Museum
from December 1998 to April 1999

First published in 1999 by British Museum Press
A division of The British Museum Company Ltd
46 Bloomsbury Street, London WC1B 3QQ

ISBN 0 7141 2542 3

A catalogue record for this book is available from the British Library

Cover Detail of a portrait of Sir Stamford Raffles by James Lonsdale
(© Zoological Society of London), inset on a detail of a Javanese royal court
sarung (BM Ethno As 1939.04.120, Raffles Collection).

Frontispiece The family crest of Sir Stamford Raffles, incorporating the Order
of the Golden Sword. This honour, conferred on Raffles by his friend, the
Sultan of Aceh, also became his ironic nickname within the East India
Company. Nowadays a version of the crest is the school badge of the Raffles
Institution of Singapore (BM Photo Service).

Designed and typeset in Caslon by John Hawkins Book Design
Printed in Great Britain by The Bath Press, Avon

CONTENTS

CONTRIBUTORS

Nigel Barley is an Assistant Keeper in the Department of Ethnography, British Museum, and author of a biographical study of Sir Stamford Raffles.

John Bastin is Reader Emeritus in the Modern History of Southeast Asia in the University of London and author of a number of books on the history of Southeast Asia, including studies of Sir Stamford Raffles.

Tim Byard-Jones holds an Oxford doctorate in Ethnomusicology as well as formal qualifications as a dhalang (puppeteer) in Yogyakarta.

Joe Cribb is an Assistant Keeper in the Department of Coins & Medals, British Museum, and author of a new study of the magic coins of Java, Bali and the Malay peninsula, based on the Raffles Collection.

Fiona Kerlogue wrote her doctorate on the batik of Jambi, Sumatra, and is a lecturer in visual anthropology at the Centre for South-East Asian Studies, University of Hull.

Jeff Roberts is a research student at the School of Oriental and African Studies, London, currently writing on the Tengger highlands.

PREFACE

The idea of an exhibition on Sir Stamford Raffles has long been in the air. It was achieved piecemeal in previous displays of the Raffles gamelan and shadow puppets at the Museum of Mankind and the notable exhibition on Raffles at the National Museum of Singapore in 1993. Practical difficulties made it impossible to stage such an exhibition to mark the fiftieth anniversary of Indonesian independence and the thirtieth year of Singaporean independence in 1995. But perhaps such anniversaries are best avoided, since they seem to appropriate too much of such a many-sided man.

The exhibition associated with this book seeks to bring together many of the diverse facets of Raffles and owes much to the generous co-operation of learned bodies with which he was involved, including the Zoological Society of London, Royal Asiatic Society and Royal Botanic Gardens at Kew, and the modern heirs to such bodies, such as the Natural History Museum, British Library and Royal Geographical Society. A special vote of thanks is due to the Raffles family for their generous co-operation in lending material, to the great disruption of their domestic quiet, and also to Standard Chartered for their generous financial support.

Raffles's contacts ranged widely, so that institutional collaborators in this project include staff of the Singapore History Museum and the Nagasaki City Museum. Numerous individuals have given indispensable assistance in the form of time and knowledge, among them Beth McKillop, Yu-Ying Brown, Annabel Teh Gallop and Janet Topp Fargion of the British Library, Michael Pollock of the Royal Asiatic Society, Ann Sylph and Richard Burge of the Zoological Society of London, Andrew Tatham of the Royal Geographical Society, and Kathie Way, Paula Jenkins and Roy Vickery of the Natural History Museum. Photographs not provided by the British Museum Photographic Service have been reproduced in this book by kind permission of the British Library, Nagasaki City Museum, National Portrait Gallery, Royal Botanic Gardens at Kew and Zoological Society of London. As usual, no Raffles project could be completed without the help of John Bastin, the doyen of Raffles studies, and I am grateful to him as well as the other contributors to this book.

It would be impossible to mention all the British Museum staff who have given of themselves to realize this exhibition and publication but invidious to mention none. Foremost, for their efforts on the book, are Joe Cribb of the Department of Coins & Medals and Nina Shandloff of British Museum Press. Thanks are also due to Richard Blurton and Robert Knox of the Department of Oriental Antiquities and Victor Harris of the Department of Japanese Antiquities for their patient support, and also to numerous colleagues in the Design Office and Department of Ethnography. Special thanks are due to Imogen Laing.

CHRONOLOGY
OF THE LIFE OF
STAMFORD RAFFLES

1781	Born off Jamaica and baptized Thomas Stamford Bingley Raffles
1795	Enters East India Company as a clerk
1805	Appointed Assistant-Secretary to Governor of Pinang and marries his first wife, Olivia
1807–8	Visits Malacca
1811	Appointed Lieutenant-Governor following British invasion of Java
1812	Institutes land reform, making East India Company the landlord of most small farmers
1814	Death of his first wife, Olivia
1815	Dismissed
1816	Returns to England
1817	Publishes *The History of Java*; knighted; marries his second wife, Sophia
1818	Leaves for Bengkulu
1819	Founds Singapore
1820	Death of his son
1822	Deaths of two further children
1823	Death of his daughter
1824	Fire and sinking of the *Fame*; returns to England
1826	Founding of the Zoological Society of London; death of Raffles
1858	Death of his second wife, Sophia, Lady Raffles

INTRODUCTION

NIGEL BARLEY

The Raffles Collection of the British Museum has long been known as the oldest systematic compilation of Indonesian material in Europe. It is distinguished not just by its antiquity but by its high aesthetic quality and by the documentation that accompanies it. Preserved primarily in Raffles's own book, *The History of Java*, this is still providing material for contemporary field research (see Chapter 6). Yet behind the seeming solidity of its name, complete with reassuring definite article, The Raffles Collection hides several other lost collections and indeed other visions of their collector (colour plate 1).

The Raffles Collection first came to the notice of the British Museum in 1859. Following the death of Sophia, Raffles's second wife, in 1858, it was offered as a possible purchase for a thousand guineas by the executors of her estate. The Keeper of the Department of Antiquities, Edward Hawkins, seems to have been enthusiastic while the Keeper of Manuscripts, Sir Frederick Madden, was not. The Trustees considered the matter at a meeting on 9 April 1859 and swiftly declined the offer. No reason was noted. On the board were figures such as the Duke of Somerset and Sir David Dundas, respectively descendants of old friends and powerful East India Company enemies of Sir Stamford, and one can only speculate on their reaction to the very name of Raffles.

But Raffles's nephew and heir, the Revd William Charles Raffles Flint, was persistent. Later in the year he wrote offering the material again, this time as a donation. He commented:

> By the death of Lady Raffles I have inherited from Sir Thomas Stamford Raffles, his valuable and interesting Collection of Javanese Antiquities and Museum illustrating the History and Customs of that Island of which he was Lt. Governor from 1811-1816. I believe the articles of which it is composed to be for the most part unique in this Country and know they were collected at much trouble and expense.
>
> His sudden and early removal shortly after his return to England in 1826 [sic],

prevented him from making any particular disposition of his Collection; I feel however that had he been permitted to do so, he would have wished the Country at large to be benefited by his labours, and I therefore feel great satisfaction in presenting it to the British Museum . . .

After some prevarication concerning who should pay the cost of transport to the Museum, the donation was accepted.

Immediately problems arose. Hawkins, the Keeper of the Department of Antiquities, regretted, 'We have not any collections with which it would be at all desirable to incorporate them.' The material ended up in a dark and ill-favoured part of the British Room. When the Reverend Raffles Flint visited the gallery in 1861, he was appalled by what he saw. 'I found the whole closely packed in a single Glass Enclosure the Wayangs piled in a heap at the bottom and the Musical Instruments set on the top whereas the former should be place against the wall singly, the latter within reach.'

Improvements were grudgingly made. But thereafter, the fate of the collection reflected not just restrictions of physical space but wider changes in the geography of knowledge as academic borders were renegotiated and objects were allocated to different spheres of interest. The collection itself was constantly redefined, as in 1866 the Department of Oriental Antiquities was established and between 1910 and 1925 that of Ceramics and Ethnography, so that the Raffles material was divided up and subdivided yet again. The basis of the partition seems to have been that material closely associated with the 'World Religions' – Islam, Hinduism, Buddhism – was assigned to Oriental Antiquities, this being another reflection of that lingering concept 'civilization', whereas Ethnography formed a residual category that absorbed everything else. It must be said that this was a distinction wholly in keeping with Raffles's own view of the matter.

Written material, including inscribed brass plaques, went to what is now the British Library. Coins and objects that were mistaken for coins found their place in the Coins & Medals Department, as described by Joe Cribb (Chapter 4). Oil paintings that formed the basis for the plates in *The History of Java* were allocated to Ethnography (colour plate 2), while similar drawings (fig. 35) and watercolours remained in Oriental Antiquities. Two Japanese masks (figs 38 and 39), previously held to be Javanese, ended up in a new Japanese Antiquities Department.

The most curious fate befell a small Javanese brass casting (Ethno 1859.12-28.102) described as 'standing nude with pigtail and monstrous face'. Although only a few centimetres high, its erect nudity was felt to make it unsuitable for public display and it was assigned to perpetual seclusion in a closed box in a locked cupboard in the *museum secretum* that otherwise housed an awkward collection of erotica.

The interests of Empire and the emphases of scholarship have associated the name of Raffles exclusively with Singapore, to the detriment of his wider researches. There is little doubt that the Raffles material has suffered from being incorporated into a larger, largely Indian collection. Even Raffles referred to Indonesia as 'this other India', as if to a derivative, marginal area. No separate British institution commemorates this omnivorous scholar and only recently was his name inscribed over the main stairs of the British Museum as a major benefactor. He has paid a high price for crossing boundaries.

A second tranche of The Raffles Collection came in 1939 from Mrs J. Drake, the great granddaughter of Raffles's heir, the Revd Raffles Flint, who had retained a small number of pieces for himself (figs 2 and 37). Some of the Borneo material, now within the collection, may actually derive from Capt. William Raffles Flint, who brought a detachment of North Borneo Company Native Police to Victoria's Diamond Jubilee in London in 1897. From stickers attached to some of these 1939 acquisitions, it appears that many had formed part of a missionary museum exhibition in Truro, organized in 1913 to raise funds for evangelization abroad.[1]

The Raffles Collection, as known, was clearly based on the large shipment of material that Raffles brought home from Java in 1816.[2] The principal motive lying behind the collection seems to have been to document the high level of Javanese civilization as an argument for the continuation of British rule. So Raffles is keen to provide his Java not just with ingenious industry and luxuriant agriculture but with an archaeology, poignant ancient ruins and parallels between 'curious' native practices and those of the classical world. The collection has determined up to the present what is the official version of Javanese material culture – masks, shadow puppets, musical instruments, stone carvings and cloth. Cloth, as Fiona Kerlogue notes (Chapter 2), is strangely absent from the Collection (but not the *History*) as we now know it, though customs records show a total of twenty-two Javanese cloths in 1816 'as Specimens for the English Manufactures'.[3] It seems they may have been sent as models to the British weaving industry, anxious to export its products to Java or – rather – by a Stamford Raffles eager to encourage such a trade to tie his beloved Java closer to Britain. They are now almost entirely lost.

Lost, too, is most of the Japanese collection (Chapter 7) that once included silk costumes, lacquerware, ceramics, swords and Japanese Christian artefacts that might have constituted an argument for maintaining the links he had created between the Company and that nation.

Theft has played its part in the whittling down of our knowledge. Family tradition has 'a hundred golden Buddhas', collected by Raffles, being stolen from Sunningdale Vicarage by a wayward servant in the late nineteenth century, so that some of those left appear of rather touristic quality. History has also voraciously swallowed up his forty-foot long replica of the Thai royal barge, shipped from Singapore in 1823, so that only a few paddles came to the British Museum.

Most disastrous of all was the destruction of the *Fame*, the vessel in which Raffles had embarked the fruits of a lifetime's collecting for the voyage from Bengkulu back to England in 1824. When it caught fire, exploded and sank (fig. 8), it transformed Raffles from the greatest benefactor of Indonesian studies into their greatest misfortune. As his protege Munshi Abdullah lamented:

> ... And when I heard this news I was breathless, remembering all the Malay books of ancient date collected from various countries – all these lost with the wonderful collection. As to his other property I do not care, for if his life was spared he could reinstate them. But the books could not be recovered for none of them were printed but in manuscript – they were so rare that one country might have two of them; that is what distressed me.[4]

Also lost, of course, was a huge natural history collection. Raffles expected to be remembered as a natural historian before anything else, and it may be argued that the pursuit of such knowledge was his foremost love. The dissolution of the East India Company Museum that housed his greatest collection and the fact that he provided other scholars so generously with types now known under their names (Chapter 1) has robbed him of the credit he deserves. But British repositories of natural history are full of unacknowledged Raffles specimens.

Indeed, it is natural history that provides the model by which we may understand all the other Raffles collections. He loved to collect things that could be arranged in sets, and certain knowledge for him came in the form of a biological taxonomy. So he homed in on the musical instruments and the various sets of puppets of the court (Chapter 3) and the gamelan orchestras (Chapter 5). He was a man absolutely not in awe of the original object but rather the information that specimens contained, so that his natural history collections abound with precise paintings by specialist Chinese artists (figs 10 and 12). Significantly, his last correspondence with Kew Gardens dealt with the making of wax models of his *Rafflesia arnoldi* Brown (colour plate 3). The small carvings of Javanese social types that he brought back (fig. 1) were little more than a substitute for collecting the species and genera of the natural domain. And in this Raffles is a man both of and before his time. While his natural history collections are striking for the number of paintings they include, his 'ethnographic collection' is full of miniature models, so that the musical instruments authoritatively illustrated in the *History* (fig. 35) are actually of doll's house proportions.

The list of specimen sentences that he sent out to be translated into the various languages of the archipelago contains the following: 'There is a country, where there is a sea, in which there is an island, in which there is a mountain, on which there is a fort, in which there is a palace, where there is a jewel of very brilliant lustre.'[5]

It is perhaps every explorer's and fieldworker's vision of the world. But for Raffles the jewel was knowledge, and he would just as soon have had a precise and serviceable copy of it as the real thing.

Fig. 1 Painted wooden figures from Java, illustrating various social types of the 19th century and used as the basis for an engraving in Raffles's *History of Java* (see colour plate 2). BM Ethno As 1859.12-28.183, 184 and 185, Raffles Collection.

Plate 1 Portrait of Sir Stamford Raffles in oils, 1817, by G. F. Joseph. On the table are Raffles's book, *The History of Java*, published in that year, and various Javanese antiquities now in the British Museum. The painting was probably commissioned to mark the knighthood conferred on Raffles by the Prince Regent, to whom the book was dedicated. Presented by Revd W. Raffles Flint, 1859. By courtesy of the National Portrait Gallery, London.

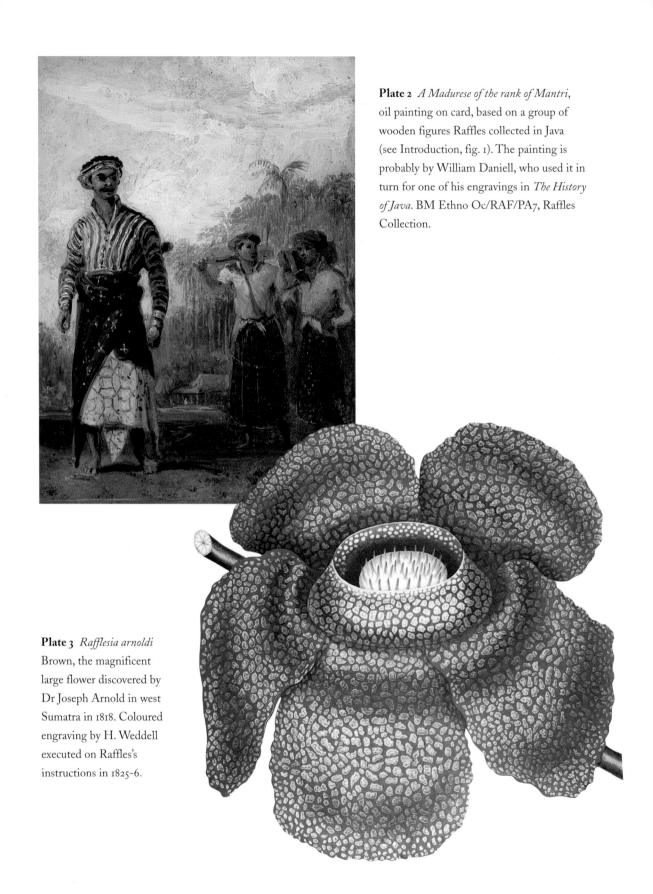

Plate 2 *A Madurese of the rank of Mantri*, oil painting on card, based on a group of wooden figures Raffles collected in Java (see Introduction, fig. 1). The painting is probably by William Daniell, who used it in turn for one of his engravings in *The History of Java*. BM Ethno Oc/RAF/PA7, Raffles Collection.

Plate 3 *Rafflesia arnoldi* Brown, the magnificent large flower discovered by Dr Joseph Arnold in west Sumatra in 1818. Coloured engraving by H. Weddell executed on Raffles's instructions in 1825-6.

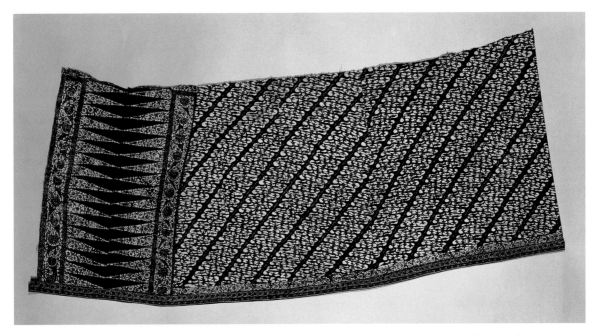

Plate 4 This sarung, decorated with the *parang rusak* design, has been cut up and reassembled so that the original direction of the pattern is no longer evident. BM Ethno 1939.As 4.119, Raffles Collection.

Plate 5 In Raffles's day the *parang rusak* design was reserved for use in the Javanese royal courts. The size of the motifs suggests that this sarung was probably intended to be worn by someone of particularly high status. BM Ethno 1939.As 4.120, Raffles Collection.

Plate 6 Metallophone *saron*, musical
instrument with twelve keys, from Java. BM Ethno As 1859.12-28.199,
Raffles Collection.

Plate 7 Woodblock print of the elephant sent by Stamford Raffles to Nagasaki in 1813. The text notes the dimensions
and weight of the beast. By permission of the Nagasaki City Museum.

Fig. 2 Wooden puppet, wayang klitik, showing a European.
BM Ethno As 1939.04.110, Raffles Collection, presented by
Mrs J. Drake.

RAFFLES THE NATURALIST

JOHN BASTIN

One of the most neglected aspects of the career of Sir Stamford Raffles in Southeast Asia is his work as a naturalist. It is well known that the giant flower *Rafflesia arnoldi* Brown (colour plate 3) is named after him and that, together with Sir Humphry Davy (fig. 4), he founded the Zoological Society of London. Otherwise, his scientific achievements have remained obscure. It is commonly supposed that his interest in natural history was aroused by his meeting with Dr Thomas Horsfield (fig. 6) in Java, after his appointment as Lieutenant-Governor of the conquered Dutch colony in 1811; but while it is true that the American naturalist was a source of inspiration to him, it is equally true that Raffles was an enthusiastic amateur naturalist before they met. Raffles's Malay scribe, Abdullah bin Abdul Kadir Munsyi, has recorded that at Melaka in 1811, when preparations were being made for the British invasion of Java, Raffles employed four men to search for specimens of natural history: 'One he told to go into the jungle and look for various kinds of leaves, flowers, fungi, mosses, and so on. Another he told to find worms, grasshoppers, various kinds of butterflies, beetles, and other different insects, cicadas, centipedes, scorpions, and the like, and he gave him some needles and told him to set the specimens. Another man he despatched with a basket to get coral, various sorts of shells, molluscs, oysters and the like, and also fish. The fourth man went out catching wild animals like birds, jungle fowl, deer, and small quadrupeds'. Raffles pressed the leaves and flowers between the pages of a large book which he kept for the purpose, while fruits and flowers were handed to a Chinese artist from Macau who made drawings of them.

It has been stated that Raffles's favourite study was botany, which he once described as 'that beautiful Science'; but his love of animals was undoubtedly greater, Lady Raffles declaring that it was 'perhaps unequalled'. In Pinang between 1805 and 1810, when he was Assistant-Secretary and later Secretary to the Prince of Wales Island government, he kept a number of animals in cages, including a siamang, and a similar specimen, which he had when he was Lieutenant-Governor of Fort Marlborough in west Sumatra, is said to have occupied more of his attention than his own children. At that time, between 1818 and 1824, he also had a Malayan Sun Bear (*Helarctos malayanus* Raffles) (fig. 9), which was brought up in the nursery with his children and often allowed to sit at his table, where it showed a marked taste for champagne. His menagerie in west Sumatra was large and included an elephant and two rusa, or deer, which had been presented to him by Sultan Ala'addin Jauhar al-Alam Syah of Aceh. Earlier, during his stay at Melaka in 1810-11, he kept at his house in Bandar Hilir, south of the town, two orang-utan, which had been given to him by the Sultan of Sambas in west Borneo, Abu Bakar Tajuddin. Also in his menagerie were a tiger, a bear and other animals, some of which had been sent to him by other Malaysian and Indonesian rulers. During his period in Java he kept two tigers at his house at Cisurua, and in 1812 he despatched to the Governor-General, Lord Minto, in Calcutta a Black Leopard (*Panthera pardus* Linnaeus), which had been caught in the eastern district of the island. His letters contain numerous references to animals, and it was his interest in them, and in zoology in general, that led him to found the Zoological Society of London, with its menagerie in Regent's Park, after he returned to London in 1824.

Raffles was also deeply interested in geology, ichthyology, entomology and virtually all branches of natural history. Its study, he believed, afforded, next to religion, 'perhaps the most rational and innocent enjoyment that Mind can possess on Earth'. After his founding of Singapore in 1819, and the curtailment of his political activities in the region, it became the principal interest of his life. 'I have thrown politics far away', he wrote to a friend in April 1820, 'and since I must have nothing more to do with men, have taken to the wilder but less sophisticated animals of our woods'. Six months earlier he had written: 'Such portion of my time as is not taken up in public business, is principally devoted to natural history. We are making very extensive collections in all departments ... '. This was, perhaps, the happiest period of Raffles's life when, after assiduous study and close associations with a number of naturalists over many years, he enjoyed the necessary leisure to engage in natural history research himself. Earlier, in Pinang and Melaka, and especially in Java, heavy administrative responsibilities had left him with few opportunities to indulge his personal interests, and he had to content himself with supporting the work of others.

Principal among these in Java was the pioneer American naturalist Dr Thomas

Horsfield (fig. 6), who had been engaged in natural history research in the island during the previous decade under the auspices of the Dutch colonial authorities. Raffles had first met him at Surakarta towards the end of 1811, and he immediately agreed to continue his official appointment. Raffles's principal objective was to secure Horsfield's large natural history collections for the British nation, and in the following year he received from the American the first collection of insects, mammalia and birds for the East India Company in London, together with various reports of his researches. These and earlier reports he arranged to have published in the *Transactions* of the Batavian Society of Arts and Sciences in Jakarta, which he had helped to reorganize. When he was about to leave Java in 1816 he invited Horsfield to accompany him to England, but the latter decided to complete his research under the newly restored Dutch government. However, he assigned all his natural history collections to the East India Company, and they were later taken by him and deposited in the Company's Museum in London.

During the fifteen months that Raffles spent in England in 1816-17, before leaving to take up the post of Lieutenant-Governor of Fort Marlborough (Bengkulu), his enthusiasm for natural history increased enormously. He met many of the leading naturalists in London and, according to Sir Joseph Banks (fig. 5), he made a great impression on them: 'We are all here delighted with the acquaintance of Governor Raffles; he is certainly among the best informed of men, and possesses a larger stock of useful talent than any other individual of my acquaintance'. With Banks's support, he persuaded the East India Company to agree to the British naval surgeon, Dr Joseph Arnold (fig. 3), accompanying him as a naturalist to Sumatra, and during the long voyage to Bengkulu he gained much from Arnold's scientific instruction. The latter's career as a naturalist in Sumatra was brief, as he died only four months after arriving in the island, but during that time he discovered, at Pulau Lebar on the Manna river in the company of Raffles, the gigantic flower (colour plate 3) of the parasitic plant to which Robert Brown assigned the generic name *Rafflesia* – 'the name I am persuaded that Dr Arnold himself would have chosen had he lived to publish an account of it ...'. Raffles thus had the good fortune to have his name associated with the prodigy of nature that was to astonish the scientific world.

After Arnold's death, Raffles appealed to Banks to use his influence with the Directors of the East India Company to secure the appointment of another naturalist to Sumatra, but nothing came of this, and it was Raffles himself who found a replacement a year later when he visited the Botanic Garden in Calcutta (Sibpur) and was introduced by the Superintendent, Dr Nathaniel Wallich (fig. 7), to a young Scottish surgeon, Dr William Jack, who was on sick leave from his regiment. Jack was only twenty-three years of age when he first met Raffles, and he died less than four years later at Bengkulu, yet he was the most gifted of all the naturalists associated with Raffles and one of the most able botanists ever to become associated with the rich flora of the Malay Archipelago. Raffles also engaged the services in Calcutta of two French zoologists, Pierre Diard and Alfred Duvaucel, the pupil and stepson, respectively, of the renowned naturalist Baron Georges Cuvier. During the voyage from Calcutta to west Sumatra, Jack and his French colleagues enjoyed an enforced period of leisure in Pinang, north Sumatra and Singapore while Raffles was engaged in official business, and they were able to commence their scientific investigations in the Malaysian region under his patronage.

These investigations continued in west Sumatra, where Diard and Duvaucel were successful in making large zoological collections, including a Malayan Tapir (*Tapirus indicus* Desmarest) (fig. 11); but the secretive attitude adopted by the French naturalists, and their refusal to honour an agreement to publish their discoveries in England, forced Raffles to seize their collections and undertake a scientific description of them himself. This 'Descriptive Catalogue', together with the collections, were shipped by Raffles to London in 1820, and established his reputation as a zoologist. Yet the collections had been made by the two Frenchmen, and the 'Descriptive Catalogue', a pioneer work in Malaysian zoology, was largely the work of William Jack. It is not clear why only Raffles's name appeared on the catalogue when it was published in the *Transactions* of the Linnean Society of London in 1821-3, but it may have had something to do with the way the collections it describes came into British hands, or possibly because Jack, as a botanist, considered it inappropriate to have his name associated with a zoological catalogue. Jack's death from pulmonary tuberculosis in September 1822 was deeply felt by Raffles, who is said to have regarded him more as a brother than a scientific assistant.

When Raffles arrived at Singapore a month after Jack's death, on his third and final visit, he had the good fortune to find Dr Nathaniel Wallich on sick leave from the Botanic Garden in Calcutta. He joined the Danish naturalist in botanical excursions on the island, and he encouraged him to establish a botanical garden in Singapore for the study of local flora and the cultivation of commercial crops. Raffles allocated an area of land on Government Hill for the purpose, and on Wallich's departure from Singapore he placed the garden under the superintendence of the Assistant Surgeon, Dr William

Montgomerie. Raffles took back with him to Bengkulu in July 1823 a variety of natural history collections from Singapore, and these and others from Sumatra, as well as a number of live animals, were loaded aboard the ship *Fame* in February 1824 for the homeward voyage to England. Tragically, barely out of sight of land, the ship was consumed by fire, with the loss of all the animals on board as well as the whole of Raffles's personal possessions and collections (fig. 8). There was, he wrote, 'scarce an unknown animal, bird, beast, or fish, or an interesting plant, which we had not on board: a living tapir, a new species of tiger, splendid pheasants, &c., domesticated for the voyage; we were, in short, in this respect a perfect Noah's ark'. Little wonder that the naturalist Sir William Jardine declared that, to natural history, 'it was the most extensive loss of materials she had ever sustained'.

Between the loss of the *Fame* and his departure from Bengkulu ten weeks later, aboard the ship *Mariner*, Raffles worked hard to replace his losses. Foremost among these was the 'superb' collection of between two and three thousand natural history drawings which, he declared, 'having been taken from life, and with scientific accuracy, were executed in a style far superior to any thing I had seen or heard of in Europe'. His Chinese artists completed during this short period some 91 drawings – 44 representing birds, 7 of mammals and 40 of plants – which are now in the British Library (figs 10, 11 and 12). He also collected during this time a variety of plants, birds and live animals, including a Clouded Leopard (*Neofelis nebulosa* Griffith) which survived the voyage but died six weeks later. In London, Raffles enlisted support for the establishment of a zoological society 'bearing the same relations to Zoology as a science, that the Horticultural Society does to Botany'. In this enterprise he was supported by Sir Humphry Davy and members of the Zoological Club of the Linnean Society of London, among whom was Dr Thomas Horsfield, who was appointed Assistant Secretary of the new Society when it came into existence in 1826, with Raffles as its first President. Land was obtained in Regent's Park for the Society's menagerie, and plans were made for a museum and library. During the course of these activities Raffles died at his house 'High Wood', in Middlesex, but the Society he founded continued to flourish and represents his greatest achievement as a naturalist.

Fig. 3 Dr Joseph Arnold (1782–1818), the British naval surgeon who accompanied Raffles to Sumatra as a naturalist and who discovered the large parasitic plant *Rafflesia arnoldi* Brown. Miniature portrait dated 1817. © Royal Botanic Gardens, Kew.

Fig. 4 Sir Humphry Davy (1778-1829), inventor of the safety-lamp, who assisted Raffles in founding the Zoological Society of London. Engraving by J. Jenkins after a painting by James Lonsdale.

Fig. 5 Sir Joseph Banks (1743-1820), President of the Royal Society, who supported Raffles's natural history research in Sumatra. Engraving by C.E. Wagstaff after a painting by Thomas Phillips.

Fig. 6 Dr Thomas Horsfield (1773-1859), American naturalist and Keeper of the East India Company Museum, London, whose research in Indonesia was supported by Raffles. Lithograph by Day & Haghe, London, after a drawing by T. Erxleben.

Fig. 7 Dr Nathaniel Wallich (1785-1854), Danish naturalist and the Superintendent of the Calcutta Botanic Garden, who helped Raffles establish the Botanic Garden in Singapore. Lithograph by M. Gauci after a portrait by Andrew Robertson.

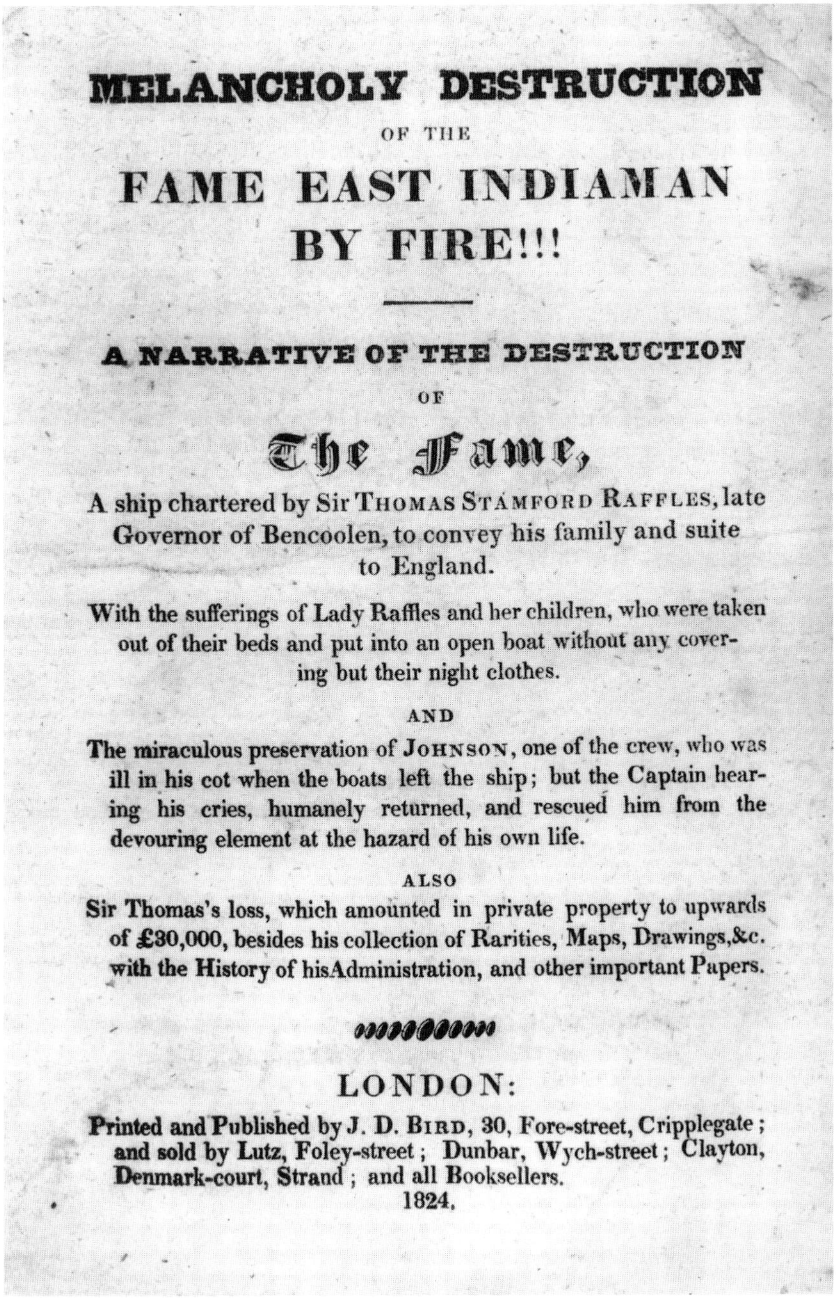

MELANCHOLY DESTRUCTION

OF THE

FAME EAST INDIAMAN
BY FIRE!!!

———

A NARRATIVE OF THE DESTRUCTION

OF

𝕿𝖍𝖊 𝕱𝖆𝖒𝖊,

A ship chartered by Sir THOMAS STAMFORD RAFFLES, late
Governor of Bencoolen, to convey his family and suite
to England.

With the sufferings of Lady Raffles and her children, who were taken
out of their beds and put into an open boat without any covering but their night clothes.

AND

The miraculous preservation of JOHNSON, one of the crew, who was
ill in his cot when the boats left the ship; but the Captain hearing his cries, humanely returned, and rescued him from the
devouring element at the hazard of his own life.

ALSO

Sir Thomas's loss, which amounted in private property to upwards
of £30,000, besides his collection of Rarities, Maps, Drawings,&c.
with the History of hisAdministration, and other important Papers.

〰〰〰〰〰〰

LONDON:

Printed and Published by J. D. BIRD, 30, Fore-street, Cripplegate;
and sold by Lutz, Foley-street; Dunbar, Wych-street; Clayton,
Denmark-court, Strand; and all Booksellers.
1824.

Fig. 8 Title page of a rare pamphlet, published in London in 1824, containing Raffles's
account of the destruction of the ship *Fame*, with the loss of his natural history and
other collections.

Fig. 9 Malayan Sun Bear (*Helarctos malayanus* Raffles), coloured aquatint by William Daniell, after a specimen sent to London from Sumatra in 1820 by Raffles, and published in Thomas Horsfield's *Zoological Researches in Java, and the Neighbouring Islands* (London, 1821-4).

Fig. 10 Durian (*Durio zibethinus, Bombacaceae*). Watercolour drawing by a Chinese artist for Raffles at Bengkulu, west Sumatra, in 1824. British Library, NHD 48. By permission of The British Library.

Fig. 11 Malayan Tapir (*Tapirus indicus* Desmarest). Watercolour drawing of a juvenile Malayan Tapir by J. Briois(?) for Raffles at Bengkulu, west Sumatra, in 1824. British Library, NHD 47. By permission of The British Library.

Fig. 12 Cashew nut (*Ancardium occidentale*). Watercolour drawing by a Chinese artist for Raffles at Bengkulu, west Sumatra, in 1824. British Library, NHD 48. By permission of The British Library.

Batik: The Cloth of Kings

FIONA KERLOGUE

Although batik from Java is nowadays famous throughout the world, until Raffles's *History of Java* was published in 1817, little was known in Europe of the art of batik. His description of the hand-drawn Javanese batik-making process shows that it has changed little since his day. A design is drawn onto the starched cloth with hot wax by means of a *canting*, a small copper vessel with a narrow spout and attached to a short bamboo handle. The pattern is drawn on both sides of the cloth, which is then immersed in a dye bath. As Raffles explained:

> The parts covered with wax resist the operation of the dye, and when the wax is removed, by steeping in hot water until it melts, are found to remain in their original condition. If the pattern is only intended to consist of one colour besides white, the operation is here completed; if another colour is to be added, the whole of the first ground, which is not intended to receive an additional shade, is covered with wax, and a similar process is repeated.[1]

Raffles reported that the waxing process might take up to seventeen days. Batik-making was carried out both in the villages and in court circles. For the dyeing, natural materials were used, such as indigo for blue and the inner bark of the root of the *mengkudu* tree for red. A final dye bath was often made from *kayu tegerang* or *kayu tingi*, wood dyes which gave a brown or reddish-brown colour known as *soga* to the parts not covered in wax. Combined with indigo, the result was almost black. In the countryside, where women produced batik cloths largely for local use, the cotton cloth was relatively coarse and the waxing crude. Court batik was worked on more finely woven cloths, and the ability to produce intricate patterns was regarded as an essential accomplishment amongst aristocratic women. It came to be regarded as a central element in the education of the princesses, teaching them patience and diligence, as well as respect for the philosophical and aesthetic values contained in the various motifs.

One of his concerns while he was in Java was to make the acquisition of Java for Britain justifiable in economic terms. His chief interest in this connection was agricultural production on the island itself, but he also turned his attention to possible markets for British products, among them textiles. In January 1813 he wrote to his friend William Ramsay about the possibility of exporting printed cottons from England to Java. His awareness of the importance of design in the eyes of local purchasers was clear: he was sanguine of success 'provided strict attention be paid to patterns and sizes'.[2] To assist the English manufacturers in adapting their styles to local taste he arranged for the collection of a set of samples, and among the items which he brought back from Java in 1816 were '22 pieces of Java cloths intended as specimens for the English Manufactures'.[3] In the past it has been assumed that two batik textiles, donated to the British Museum in 1939 by descendants, were the only remaining survivors of this collection (colour plates 4 and 5). However, a close examination of the cloths reveals that they have a different origin.

In 1749 there had been a split in the ruling family of the kingdom of Mataram, which had its capital at Surakarta in Central Java. The ruler, or Susuhunan, Paku Buwono II, had signed an agreement with the Dutch East India Company, the VOC, in which he had ceded the territory of the kingdom to the Dutch. On his death, the Dutch crowned his heir as the new king, with the title Paku Buwono III. However, several princes supported the old sultan's younger brother, Prince Mangkubumi, and after a bitter struggle, the Mataram kingdom was divided into two principalities: the kingdom of Surakarta and the kingdom of Yogyakarta. The Sultan of the newly formed kingdom of Yogyakarta was determined that his kingdom should equal that of Surakarta, with an artistic and cultural style at the same time based on tradition but distinct from that of Surakarta. Batik was one of the arts which he encouraged at court, and this was to have its own distinctive character. For example, while both courts used the *parang rusak* ('broken knife') design in their sarungs, the pattern in Yogyakarta batik ran in the opposite direction to that of Surakarta, in which it ran from the upper right to the lower left part of the cloth. The background of Yogyakarta cloth was to be white, as opposed to the creamy beige of Surakarta batik.[4]

The two batik cloths which were donated to the British Museum in 1939 are both skirt cloths originally sewn into a tube and known as *sarungs*.[5] They might have been worn by a man or a woman. They are both in the style of the Central Javanese courts, decorated with the parang rusak design, a motif which was considered sacred, and which could only be worn by the Sultan and members of his immediate family. This rule had been introduced not long before Raffles's visit, when both the Susuhunan of Surakarta, Paku Buwono III, and the ruler and founder of the neighbouring sultanate of Yogyakarta, now entitled Sultan Hamengku Buwono I, had decreed that certain designs were forbidden to those outside the aristocracy. The motifs were symbolic, the parang rusak design signifying power, authority and nobility. Portraits of members of the royal family now hanging in the *kraton*, the royal palace, suggest that the design worn by the ruler himself had the largest motifs; the queen, princes and princesses would wear similar designs, but with smaller motifs.

The two cloths in the British Museum are probably among the earliest examples of Javanese batik in any collection. Both consist of a main panel, or *kepala*, made up of triangular motifs with vertical panels to either side, and a main body, or *badan*, on which the parang rusak design has been drawn. The cloths have been dyed first in indigo and then in a soga bath. Of the two, the sarung with the smaller motifs (colour plate 4) is in many ways the more interesting. It is worked on quite finely woven material, with a thread count of between 30 and 45 threads per cm. The background is white, but as in the second cloth (colour plate 5), some parts of the wax have been deliberately cracked before the final brown dye bath, allowing the soga to seep in and give a bronze marbled effect. At some point in its history, whether in Java or in later years in England, the cloth has been cut up into four pieces and reassembled so that it is no longer possible to be certain in which way the diagonal lines originally ran. It may be that the retailored cloth was then gathered and made into a skirt; there is a dart in one of the panels indicating an attempt to make it into a fitted garment. A narrow border from another piece of Javanese cloth has been added and sewn along the lower edge of the cloth, perhaps to add to its length for a particular wearer, or perhaps just as a decorative trim. It may be that the skirt was worn at a fancy dress ball.

The other sarung with the larger motifs (colour plate 5) was clearly once sewn into a tube to make a sarung, but it has now been unstitched. The cloth is much coarser than in the previous piece, with a thread count of only 22 per cm in the weft and 25 per cm in the warp. What is interesting about this cloth, though, is that the diagonal lines of the parang rusak design run from the upper left to the lower right edge of the cloth. This and its white background clearly mark it as a piece from the Yogyakarta court.

The fact that batiks are both worked in the royal parang rusak design is intriguing. Textiles were often given to visiting dignitaries, but it may at first seem surprising that a cloth with a motif restricted to royalty should have been given to a European. However, a ceremonial dagger, or *kris*, was sometimes given on such occasions, and since there were also strict rules about who had the right to wear a kris, and a similar belief in its protective power, the giving of either of these gifts would have had a similar significance. By the time of his departure from Java, Raffles was revered as a powerful and almost supernatural figure, precisely the sort of personage on whom such a distinguished and symbolic gift might have been bestowed. The question then is who gave the batiks to Raffles, and when.

According to the journal of Captain Thomas Travers, who served as Assistant Secretary during the military operations against Yogyakarta and later as his aide-de-camp, Sultan Hamengku Buwono II of Yogyakarta was in 1811 'the most violent and intriguing of the native princes of Java [and] entertained a rooted animosity against all the Europeans settled in the island'.[6] When Raffles first received a visit from the Sultan of Yogyakarta in December 1811, the Sultan was 'accompanied by several thousands of armed followers, who expressed in their behaviour an infuriated spirit of insolence; and several of his own suite actually unsheathed their creesses, to indicate plainly that they only waited for the signal to perpetrate the work of destruction'.[7] It is clearly unlikely that Raffles would have been presented with such a gift on that occasion.

In June 1812, however, the British deposed the Sultan and installed his heir in his place, as Hamengku Buwono III. Relations with the new Sultan were more cordial, and in December of 1813, Raffles paid him a state visit, accompanied by his wife Olivia. This time Raffles was received with great pomp and ceremony. According to the *Java Government Gazette* of 8 January 1814, 'this meeting was rendered truly interesting by the gratitude and unaffected pleasure manifested by H.H. the Sultan'. The visit lasted several days, and included a tour of the Water Palace for Lieutenant-Governor Raffles and Olivia, followed by a reception in the Sultan's private apartments.[8] It is possible that the two batiks were presented as a pair to the couple on this visit, and if they were intended for Raffles and Olivia, then this is the most likely occasion. Another possibility, however, is that they may have been presented to Raffles in January 1816, a year after Olivia's death, when he paid visits first to the Susuhunan of Surakarta and then to the eleven-year-old Hamengku Buwono IV, who had succeeded his father as Sultan of Yogyakarta in November 1814. After witnessing tiger and buffalo fights in the kraton,

Raffles and his party returned to the English Residency, where Thomas Travers reports that he was given a kris and a piece of cloth 'such as is worn by the royal family' by Prince Paku Alam.[9] It seems more than likely that a similar gift would have been made to Raffles.

It is possible that Raffles acquired the two batiks separately, and he may originally have had many more. However, the fact that these are the only two to remain, and that one has a small design and the other a large one, does suggest that they were given to Raffles as a pair on an occasion when Olivia was present. They would certainly have made a highly suitable gift for the couple. The batik with the smaller design might have been intended for Olivia, while the larger design would have been commensurate with higher status. If these cloths were indeed royal gifts intended personally for the couple, then this would explain why they alone survived of the batiks which Raffles brought back to England.

Fig. 13 Wooden Javanese puppet of a unique type but resembling wayang golek, showing parang rusak designs on the batik cloth. BM Ethno As 1859.12-28.439, Raffles Collection.

THE RAFFLES
WAYANG PUPPETS

TIM BYARD-JONES

The shadow theatre of Java, known as *wayang kulit* (literally 'leather shadows'), is arguably the most complex and highly developed of all varieties of shadow theatre, an art form found from Turkey in the West to Bali in the East and which forms a major element of many Southeast Asian cultures. Wayang, regarded as the principle art form in Javanese puppetry, has influenced dance styles, helped to shape much in Javanese music and poetry and is regularly referred to in conversation and journalism to comment on current events.

Following his usual omnivorous interest in Javanese culture, Raffles acquired a substantial number of leather puppets (figs 14, 15 and 16) during his time in Java. The Raffles puppets come from two different genres of wayang: *wayang purwa* and *wayang madya*. Wayang purwa ('original' wayang) is the main classical form, and uses stories taken from the great Sanskrit epics of the Mahabharata and Ramayana, while wayang madya ('middle' wayang) is used to present stories taken from the medieval Javanese romances about the princes Panji and Damarwulan. Wayang purwa is by far the most popular genre of wayang, and seems to have been so from at least the Middle Ages. Neither group of puppets constitutes a complete set – which is unsurprising considering that some of the royal palace sets consist of more than a thousand separate puppets – but all the major character types and design features are represented.

In Java, wayang performances are normally sponsored to celebrate a particular event such as a circumcision ceremony. At the performance venue, a white cotton screen will be set up, behind which hangs a lamp, traditionally an oil lamp but nowadays usually electric. Along the bottom of the screen runs a banana tree log, the spongy fibres of which provide a stage into which the sharpened control rods of the puppets can be pushed. A performance takes all night, starting at around 9 pm and continuing until dawn.

During the performance, the puppeteer – known as a *dhalang* – not only manipulates the dozens of puppets needed for the performance but provides them with voices, sings mood-setting songs, directs the accompanying gamelan orchestra, improvizes around the basic storyline and entertains the audience with topical humour. Wayang is traditionally described as *Saptamuka*, i.e. 'Seven-faced', combining the arts of vocal music, instrumental music, literature, story-telling, carving, painting and puppet manipulation. Behind the dhalang is a gamelan orchestra, which plays throughout the performance: slow stately classical compositions for kings, fast dramatic pieces for fight sequences, and soft accompaniment for the dhalang's singing.

The origins of wayang are obscure, but the earliest reference to a wayang performance in Javanese literature is datable to AD 907. Unfortunately, we have no idea of the details of these early performances and no surviving puppets. Some light on the nature of pre-Islamic wayang is shed by Balinese wayang, which may preserve some older stylistic elements, but almost the first reliable description we have is that written by Raffles in *The History of Java*.

One of the most striking elements of any wayang kulit performance is the beauty of the leather puppets themselves, not only the few dozen used in the performance but the dozens more (sometimes hundreds) arrayed to either side of the screen (*simpingan*). Carved in incredible detail and painted with gold, black, red, white and other colours, they provide the main visual aesthetic experience of the performance. The details of puppet design vary from region to region within Java, with the most elaborate puppets being found in the Yogyakarta-Surakarta area.

Though there is no record of exactly where or from whom Raffles obtained his puppets, they clearly belong to the Central Javanese style of wayang and were probably made somewhere in the Yogyakarta-Surakarta area.

The Raffles puppets are particularly interesting to students of wayang for a number of reasons. First and most important, they can be dated with reasonable certainty, unlike most major sets in Java which have had puppets repaired and replaced frequently over the years. Second, evidence of wear shows that the puppets were used in performances for a considerable time before Raffles acquired them, rather than being specially made for him. They thus give a unique insight into the nature of the puppets used in wayang performances two hundred years ago. The most striking thing about them as a set is how similar they are to the puppets used in wayang purwa today – all the puppets are instantly recognizable to anyone familiar with contemporary wayang.

Traditional wayang performances take approximately nine hours, from around 9 pm to dawn, and are divided into three sections: *pathet nem*, *pathet sanga* and *pathet manyura*. The dramatic pattern is always the same, regardless of the story being told, and likewise many of the accompanying gamelan pieces will always be used whatever the story. The first scene of pathet nem is always set in the audience hall of a king and involves the king himself, other members of the royal family, courtiers and diplomats. The main point of this scene is first to establish the background for the plot and second to demonstrate the dhalang's command of court/literary Javanese. During this scene some news is delivered which requires action, and (usually) the army prepares for a campaign. This is often followed by another audience-hall scene in the 'opposing' court. A series of inconclusive fights usually rounds off pathet nem.

Pathet sanga normally opens with the four clown servants (*panakawan*) waiting for their master to arrive. The panakawan are among the most important characters in wayang. Semar is the incarnation of the guardian spirit of Java itself (some sources have Semar as a Hindu god), and he is accompanied by his three sons Gareng, Petruk and Bagong. The panakawan always appear as servants of the hero of the story. The hero then sets out and meets the demon Cakil, whom he kills. He then encounters the problem outlined in pathet nem, and solves it during pathet manyura.

Wayang characters are divided broadly into seven types: *halus* (refined males), *gagah* (vigorous males), *gusen* (coarse), *putri* (women), *danawa* (ogres), *wanara* (monkeys) and *dhagelan* (clowns). In addition to these, there are puppets representing the tree of life (*kayon*), various animals (horses, elephants, tigers etc.) and props (the tree of life, swords, arrows, daggers, letters etc.). There are substantial differences in size as well as form: generally speaking, danawa are the largest, gagah and wanara are next, followed by gusen, halus and putri puppets. Dhagelan vary greatly, from Petruk, who is as tall as some gagah puppets, to Sarawita, one of the shortest of all characters. This classification of character types applies not only to puppet design but also to accompanying gamelan pieces, terms of address used in dialogue, puppet movement and voice characterization.

Wayang kulit puppets are carved, using a hammer and chisels, from one or more pieces of buffalo hide, the exact number depending on how many movable parts the arms have. The arms are fixed with rivets, traditionally made from buffalo bone. The hide has to be prepared for up to a year before carving can start, and takes the form of parchment rather than leather. Old puppets, particularly those from the *pusaka* (sacred heirloom) sets in the royal palaces, are often copied. After carving (which can take anything from a few hours to a few weeks, depending on the size and complexity) the puppet is painted. Then a central supporting rod (*gapit*) is fashioned from buffalo horn, which is first softened over a flame to allow it to be stretched and bent to the shape required. Similar control rods (*tuding*) are attached to the arms. The best-quality rods are made from the horns of the albino buffalo, which is translucent.

For classical wayang purwa puppets, both the carving and the painting are constrained by the limitations of tradition, although newer forms of wayang can give a puppet maker – as well as the dhalang and musicians – more scope for originality. It is this creative freedom which is behind the development of most if not all variant forms of wayang, including wayang madya, although none of these variant forms have ever seriously challenged the popularity of wayang purwa.

Like the figures in ancient Egyptian paintings, wayang figures appear at first to be in an impossible position: the eye is seen from the front, the face in profile, arms and legs from the side but the torso from the front. Put aside the idea that this is supposed to be a picture of a real person – a wayang puppet is better thought of as being a sequence of pieces of graphic code in which each element of the body is seen in its most characteristic form or appearance, in order to present the maximum amount of information about the character represented.

Some wayang characters are instantly recognizable (e.g. the panakawan or the demon Cakil), others are familiar through popularity (e.g. the Pandawa brothers or the monkey Hanoman), for some the distinguishing elements must be learned (e.g. differentiating the twins Nakula and Sadewa in the Mahabharata from the twins Guwarsa and Guwarsi in the Ramayana). Needless to say, this greater depth of knowledge is irrelevant for anyone other than the dhalang and those assisting him directly in sorting out puppets or setting up the simpingan, since the identity of the puppets used during the performance will be clear from the context.

Halus and putri characters, for instance, have a very narrow and elongated eye, while gagah characters have round eyes. Demons and monkeys have both eyes represented on the puppet, unlike human characters who always have only one eye visible. The demon Cakil has only one eye visible, but it is crescent-shaped. Similar differences in hairstyles, head-dresses, costume details, body details, arm and leg adornments and hand positions distinguish character types and individual characters from each other.

Body colour also implies something about character: white means holiness or purity, gold is for nobility, black represents resolution or forthrightness, pink or red implies a quick temper, blue means cruelty and green shows deceitfulness. Some characters will be represented by several different puppets in different colours or forms. For example, a major character such as Arjuna (the third of the Pandawa brothers, who are the heroes of the Mahabharata) will normally be represented in a set of wayang figures by about a dozen separate puppets, representing Arjuna at various stages of his life: the young Arjuna is known as Janaka, Permadi and Mintaraga at various stages, and puppets representing these phases have extravagant arm and leg adornments and, in the case of Mintaraga, waist-length hair. On gaining maturity, however, Arjuna dispenses with this ostentation, and the adult Arjuna is plainly dressed with no adornments whatsoever. Similarly, different coloured versions of the same character can help to indicate mood, an obvious example being the contrast between Bima (the second of the Pandawa), with a gold body and black face, and Bima, who has a black body and black face – the latter is more forthright (i.e. short-tempered and provocative) than the former.

While on the subject of stylization, it is interesting to note that in Bali – where many pre-Islamic Javanese cultural elements have been preserved – the puppets are a great deal less stylized than in Java today. Javanese tradition attributes this to Kyai Sunan Kalijaga, one of the *wali sanga* (the nine Islamic saints who brought Islam to Java). Realizing that he would never wean the Javanese off wayang but finding it difficult to reconcile this with the Muslim prohibition on representative art, he introduced the extreme stylization as a way of getting round the problem, and even used wayang as a vehicle for Muslim preaching. So successful was this approach that some Muslim Javanese even credit Sunan Kalijaga with the creation of wayang theatre itself, ascribing Muslim theological elements to the stories and claiming, for instance, that the five Pandawa brothers of the Mahabharata represent the five principles of Islam.

One question frequently asked by newcomers to the world of wayang is why the puppets are painted, if all the audience can see is the shadows. This has confused a number of non-Javanese commentators over the years. One authority suggested that men sit on the dhalang's side of the screen, where they can see the colours, while women are confined to the shadow side. Another suggested that invited guests sit on the dhalang's side, while uninvited guests sit on the shadow side. While it is true that the audience at a modern wayang performance is spread out on both sides of the screen, there is no hard and fast rule for who sits where: people go where there is room for them, where they can get a good view or wherever they like. In any case, many of the colours do show through the screen, given good enough buffalo hide to start with and a strong enough light. Dhalangs going to see other dhalangs perform invariably sit on the dhalang's side of the screen.

While wayang is still a healthy and popular art form in Java itself, despite the popularity of television and cinema, wayang performances require a little work for outsiders to truly appreciate. Much of the first pathet consists of static dialogue in high Javanese, during which the dhalang demonstrates his knowledge of courtly forms of address and linguistic politeness. Needless to say, to a non-Javanese audience this is incomprehensible and extremely boring. Another problem is that, over the course of a nine-hour performance, a Javanese audience does not sit still and concentrate on the action as a Western theatre audience would (at least in theory). Instead food is served, people move around and there is an underlying buzz of conversation. Things get a bit more lively around midnight, when the clowns come on, but even then most of the humour is in Javanese. As Raffles perhaps appreciated, the most accessible aspect of wayang is the beauty of the puppets themselves, which can be enjoyed as works of art outside the performance context.

Wayang today is constantly evolving new styles and genres, and new musical pieces and puppet moves are being added to the core repertoire. New media are changing the way dhalangs are evaluated: the coming of radio and cassette recordings brought about a greater appreciation of dhalangs with particularly fine singing voices, while today televized wayang performances help to popularize dhalangs famous for their skills in puppet movement. Electric light has replaced the traditional oil lamp, and amplification allows dhalangs to make themselves heard by larger audiences and over a larger accompanying gamelan – in the last century there would have been eight or ten accompanying musicians, whereas nowadays a popular dhalang may be accompanied by thirty or forty.

Yet, despite all these changes, the core repertoire of wayang stories and performance styles is recognizably the same today as it was when it caught the attention of Raffles two hundred years ago, and anyone who truly wishes to understand Javanese culture is still well advised to get to know wayang purwa.

Fig. 14 Leather shadow puppet, wayang purwa, shown in silhouette and representing Raden (Prince) Wara Kasuma. BM Ethno As 1859.12-28.497, Raffles Collection.

Fig. 15 Leather shadow puppet, wayang purwa, showing a horse. BM Ethno As 1859.12-28.584, Raffles Collection.

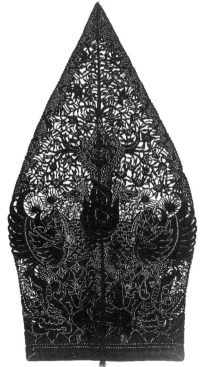

Fig. 16 Leather *gunungan*, 'cosmic mountain' form, which begins and ends the shadow play. BM Ethno As 1939.04.50, Raffles Collection.

RAFFLES'S
MAGIC COINS

JOE CRIBB

In 1835 the British Museum acquired five large square-holed bronze coins which had been brought back from Java among the thirty tons of material collected by Raffles during his stay on the island from 1811 to 1816. These five pieces were part of the large collection of oriental coins given to the British Museum by William Marsden, a specialist in Malay studies and oriental coins and a friend of Raffles. In the catalogue of his coin collection (1823-5) Marsden stated that he had been given them and ten other examples by Raffles. He illustrated only four of the five pieces he gave to the British Museum and neither described nor illustrated the other ten.

According to Raffles's account of these coins in his *History of Java*, he had acquired 'a collection of upwards of a hundred' and brought them to England. He illustrated ten of them on a plate in the same volume (fig. 17) but, apart from the pieces given to Marsden, the collection disappeared from sight until 1859, when it was given to the British Museum along with the rest of what survived of Raffles's thirty tons. The British Museum registers for the Raffles Collection are curiously silent about this part of his collection, merely listing them as 'coins' nos 172-212 in case 8. The individual numbers appear to represent groups of coins, because along with the 'upwards of a hundred', there were also two hoards of Chinese bronze coins. No further record of the coins was made until the early 1970s when they were found in the Department of Coins & Medals, in a small box labelled 'Raffles's coins'. In the box were eight of the ten pieces illustrated in *The History of Java* (figs 18-25), together with another 98 similar pieces. Including the pieces he had given to Marsden and the two illustrated in 1817 but not given to the British Museum, Raffles's 'upwards of a hundred' totaled at least 123, of which 111 are now in the British Museum. The whereabouts of the twelve missing examples, and any others Raffles might have given away, is not known.

Two of Raffles's colleagues in Java also collected examples of these large square-holed bronze coins and brought them back to Britain. Thomas Horsfield (fig. 6), an American doctor, who worked for Raffles collecting and making drawings, recorded a small collection of eleven coins in drawings which are now in the British Library.[2] Eight of the pieces recorded by Horsfield are now in the Fitzwilliam Museum, Cambridge. John Crawfurd, a member of Raffles's staff serving as British Resident at the court of Jogjakarta, collected at least four examples. He published two in 1820 in his *History of the Indian Archipelago*, and these are now in a private collection in London. The other two were not published but were given to the British Museum in 1842.

The large square-holed bronze coins were not known to scholarship before Raffles illustrated them in 1817. They have the same shape as the Chinese bronze cash coins commonly found in Java but are generally larger: averaging about 40 mm in diameter, they are almost twice the standard size (about 23 mm) of the Chinese cash coins. They also have pictorial designs in place of the inscriptions which decorate Chinese coins.

Raffles said they were found 'in the central and eastern districts of Java, in the vicinity of dilapidated temples'. Raffles visited a number of such sites during his travels in Java, but it is not clear whether he actually found the pieces himself or gathered together examples collected by others. The latter is more likely, in view of the large number of these rare pieces he was able to assemble in less than five years. He observed that the holes in their centres were similar to those found in Chinese and Japanese coins. He described the designs as 'various subjects in relief',[3] but in his discussion of Javanese wayang shadow puppets he remarked on the coins' similarity to the puppets. He thought the coins were of Java's pre-Islamic period and that the coin designs represented evidence that the process of stylization in the puppets must therefore have begun before the Islamic period.[4]

He could not understand the designs on the coins, so he sought the assistance of one of his Javanese advisers, the Kiai Adipati of Demak (Sura Adimanggala, regent of Semarang). It appears that the Kiai Adipati understood them no better than Raffles, because the explanation he produced does not bear scrutiny. He told Raffles that the pictures were all examples of the *Chandra Sangkala*, a Javanese system of using pictures to indicate dates, and explained each of the design elements as a visual numeral, combining to indicate dates in the Javanese version of the Indian Shaka era (beginning in AD 78).

Raffles explained one of them as an example: 'Thus the last [coin on the plate (figs 17 and 25)], which has the date 1568, is explained as follows:

Naga	*hoba*	*wisaya*	*jalma*
Snakes	move	work	men
8	6	5	1

That is to say, 'snakes are moving while men are working', alluding to the two snakes which appear entwining together between and above the two men who are mastering an animal.[5]

Raffles conceded that this system 'appears so uncertain and ill understood, that perhaps but little reliance is to be placed on it'. He did, however, label the coins on his plate with the dates provided in this way, although a brief examination of the plate should have shown him that the system was not appropriate and that his hesitation in accepting it was fully justified: he illustrated two pieces with the same design (fig. 17, centre top and fourth down), giving them dates of '1068' and '1246', and gave another piece (fig. 18) two different dates ('862' and '851') for the back and front (fig. 17, left top and second down).

Some of the specimens in the British Museum have paper labels attached which show further evidence of the Kiai Adipati's explanation. A piece showing a woman with a spinning wheel, thread-winder, chicken cage, rice trough, rice kettle, dish, chicken and water pot (fig. 17, left centre, and fig. 19) is explained as dated *gedong* (building) 8, *hadie* (water) 4, *roso* (strength) 6 = 846. Another, showing a woman under a tree with spinning wheel, thread-winder, rice barn, rice kettle, rice cone, water pot and staff (fig. 17, fourth down on left, and fig. 20), is explained as dated *kendie* (water pot) 9, *banjoe* (water) 4, *roso* (strength) 6 = 946. It is difficult to see the connection between these interpretations and the designs illustrated.

Not only was Raffles mistaken to pay attention to the Chandra Sangkala, but he was also wrong to identify these objects as coins. Although the same shape as coins, they were made for entirely different reasons. Marsden and Crawfurd shared Raffles's opinion, but a Russian scholar, de Chaudoir, realized that they had a different function. He included copies of Raffles's, Marsden's and Crawfurd's illustrations[6] in the first major study in a European language of East Asian coins and recognized their similarity to Chinese and Japanese coin-shaped amulets. This resemblance was further explored in 1863 by two Dutch scholars, Netscher and van der Chijs, and in 1871 by another Dutch scholar, Millies. They considered the coins collected by Raffles and other similar examples they had recorded to be a Javanese version of Chinese coin-shaped amulets.

Netscher and van der Chijs explained the designs as representations of Javanese deities who acted as patrons of the days of the week. Millies's explanation related the images to the wayang shadow-puppet theatre and suggested that the designs represented episodes in wayang plays, but he could not identify particular puppets. He also identified some of the scenes as representations of a wedding.

An explanation of the purpose of the coins Raffles collected did not emerge until 1936, when Rentse, a student of Malay magic, published an account of similar large coin-shaped pieces being used among the Javanese community in Kelantan in the Malay Peninsula. In the early 1930s he collected some examples and saw one being used by a local 'medicine man' in an exorcism ceremony. He identified the figures depicted on the pieces in his collection as characters in a version of the Javanese wayang shadow-puppet theatre called *wayang gedog*. On one side he recognized the hero of wayang gedog, the prince Panji, and his wife Candra Kirana, and on the other Panji's servants, the *panakawan* puppets Bancak and Doyok (fig. 26). He described how the 'medicine man' used the coin-shaped pieces not 'as currency, but purely for magical purposes' as a substitute for the puppets depicted on it, to perform a ritual wayang performance, regularly performed in the Javanese community as a guard against evil spirits. He suspended it on a string in incense smoke and asked the 'gods' represented to descend through the smoke and effect the exorcism.

The images on Rentse's 'magic coins' were versions of the puppets of Panji (fig. 29), his wife (fig. 30) and servants (figs 31 and 32) as represented in the Raffles Collection. When compared with the large coin-shaped pieces in Raffles's coin collection, some similarities can be seen. The most common designs on the front show a noble man and woman in wayang style standing beneath a tree. On some examples there are servant figures with the features of Bancak and Doyok on the back (fig. 25). The man and woman wear the same clothes and ornaments as Raffles's puppets of Panji and Candra Kirana, but they have a different hair style, with a long forelock. This forelock can, however, be identified as the distinguishing feature of Panji in Balinese art. It is clear that the makers of the magic coins collected by Rentse were copying designs from pieces like those collected by Raffles, recognizing that they depicted an earlier version of Panji than was available when Raffles collected his puppets.

In the 1930s another eyewitness described the use of magic coins with designs like those on the pieces in Raffles's coin collection. Covarrubias's account of his visit to Bali[7] described the use of large square-holed coins with images of puppets as love-charms.

The owner of such a magic coin considered that it gave him the power of the hero Arjuna, whose puppet was depicted on it, to gain many lovers. The accuracy of this report was confirmed in the 1970s by a similar account given to Hobart, a researcher into Balinese wayang. Hobart's account mentioned magic coins with various designs, each bringing its owner the powers of the puppet depicted on it. One of these magic coins, with an image of the servant puppet Tualen (the Balinese version of Bancak), could be used by a medicine man to drive out evil spirits.

The common tradition among the Javanese in Kelantan and the Balinese suggests that the use of these magic coins can be traced back to an earlier period of Javanese history when contacts between Java and Bali were closer. The tradition of using magic coins must originate before the time of Raffles's stay in Java, when they had already become antiquities to be dug up 'in the vicinity of dilapidated temples'. Raffle presumed this meant they should be dated to the pre-Islamic period, i.e. before the sixteenth century.

The shape of the magic coins collected by Raffles and still in use when Rentse collected them was that of Chinese cash coins. It seems likely that the shape was copied from Chinese coins, imported into Java in large numbers from the late thirteenth century, which were the official currency of the Majapahit empire of East Java during the fourteenth and fifteenth centuries.

No surviving wayang puppets can be identified as older than the examples collected by Raffles, so it is difficult to compare the images on the magic coins with puppets of the Majapahit period (1293-1528). There are, however, stone reliefs surviving on Hindu monuments in East Java which give some indication that wayang puppets were popular from the early fourteenth century and that from the middle of the century they often featured puppets of servant figures. The representation of Panji's servant Bancak on some magic coins in the Raffles Collection is very similar to the servant figures depicted in stone reliefs of the Majapahit period (fig. 33). On some of these reliefs there are also representations of Panji, showing him wearing the same long forelock featured on the magic coins. On the basis of this similarity, it seems likely that the tradition of using magic coins in Java can be traced back to the Majapahit period. Some examples may be as early as the beginning of that period.

Similar representations of figures in an early wayang style are also found on a group of Majapahit bronze 'zodiac beakers' (fig. 28) now in the British Museum Department of Oriental Antiquities, which can be dated to the fourteenth century by dates inscribed on some examples. A beaker in the Stuttgart Linder Museum is decorated with an impression of a magic coin.[8] It is typical of the East Javanese zodiac beakers, which have been known since Raffles's publication (fig. 27) of two examples.[9] Such beakers are still in use in Tengger, East Java[10] and Bali.[11] The designs are in the wayang style and not dissimilar in treatment of wayang figures to Raffles's magic coins. The Stuttgart zodiac beaker, like some others, has a date below the rim on the outside. The date is 1253 in the Indian Shaka era, equivalent to AD 1331. The recorded dates on similar beakers are mostly in the mid-fourteenth century, beginning (fig. 28, left) with 1251 (AD 1329),[12] but later dates are reported and an example in use in Bali bears the date 1427 (i.e. AD 1505).[13]

The representations of Panji and his wife on the front of many of the magic coins collected by Raffles shows them under a *waringin* fig tree, with domestic objects by their feet, in an image which appears to represent their wedding. Raffles quotes a traditional Javanese wedding prayer expressing the hope that the bride and groom will flourish like the waringin tree.[14] Raffles describes some of the domestic objects depicted by their feet as traditional Javanese wedding gifts: implements for preparing food and drink, such as chicken cage, chicken and egg, rice barn, rice-pounding trough, rice steamer and rice cone, gridiron, water pot and dish, and implements for making cloth such as spinning-wheel and thread-winder. On the back of most of these magic coins Panji's wife is shown surrounded by the same domestic implements. On a few examples, however, Panji is shown with whip, bull (fig. 23) and plough (fig. 24), which are also described by Raffles as wedding gifts,[15] or he is depicted on horseback, riding to his wedding.[16]

The representation of Panji and Candra Kirana at their wedding seems to be intended as a powerful symbol against evil spirits. It is an invocation of the couple as they become the ancestors, and therefore the guardians, of the Javanese people.

The role of Panji and Candra Kirana in exorcism is reinforced in two ways. Their representation as wayang figures refers to the performance of wayang plays as a means of keeping away evil spirits. The wedding gifts shown around their feet are similar to the ritual offerings made in Java and Bali during preparations for ceremonies, such as weddings and funerals, to ward off evil forces.

Two of the representations on the magic coins illustrated by Raffles which do not have a direct relationship with the wedding of Panji and Candra Kirana can also be interpreted as rituals relating to exorcism. The first piece on Raffles's plate (fig. 17, top left, and fig. 18) shows Panji crouched inside a chicken cage. Rentse describes this position being adopted by a wayang puppet-master as he prepares to perform a wayang play for an exorcism.[17] The last piece on Raffles's plate (fig. 17, bottom right, and fig. 25) shows Panji's servants Bancak and Doyok sacrificing a bull. In Bali and East Java bulls are only sacrificed in preparation for important ceremonies, as an offering to keep evil spirits away.

Although Raffles had no idea what he was preserving, he recognized the antiquity and historical value of his magic coins, and he assembled a large enough number of them to enable the reports of twentieth-century eye-witnesses to be interpreted as evidence of a traditional use of coin-shaped amulets reaching back into Java's pre-Islamic period. The representations of wayang puppets on the magic coins provide, as Raffles realized, important evidence of the evolution of the puppets' style during the period before the earliest surviving examples in Raffles's own collection.

Fig. 17 Raffles's coins, on the plate opposite p. 60 in *The History of Java*, vol. 2.

Raffles's coins in the British Museum (see fig. 17), from left to right:

Fig. 18, *front*: Panji and Candra Kirana standing under waringin tree with wedding gifts; *back*: Panji in chicken cage (Cribb 1999, no. 43a).

Fig. 19, *front*: Candra Kirana with wedding gifts; *back*: blank (Cribb 1999, no. 64a).

Fig. 20, *front:* Panji and Candra Kirana sitting under waringin tree with wedding gifts; *back*: Candra Kirana under waringin tree with wedding gifts (Cribb 1999, no. 110a).

Raffles's coins in the British Museum (see fig. 17), from left to right:
Figs 21 and 22, *front*:Panji and Candra Kirana standing under waringin tree with wedding gifts;
back: Candra Kirana with wedding gifts (Cribb 1999, nos 21e and 21b).
Fig. 23, *front*: Panji and Candra Kirana standing under spinning wheel with wedding gifts;
back: Panji with whip, bull, chicken, dog and deer (Cribb 1999, no. 58a).

Raffles's coins in the British Museum (see fig. 17), from top to bottom (90 per cent of actual size):
Fig. 24, *front*: Panji with whip, bull, chicken and plough;
back: Candra Kirana's servant with wedding gifts (Cribb 1999, no. 42a).
Fig. 25, *front*: Panji and Candra Kirana standing under waringin tree with wedding gifts;
back: Panji's servants, Bancak (left) and Doyok, sacrificing bull, with snakes above (Cribb 1999, no. 103b).

Fig. 26 Modern version of magic coin, made *c.* 1930 in Kelantan, Malaya; *front*: Panji and Candra Kirana standing under waringin tree, with spinning wheel, chicken and elephant; *back*: Panji's servants, Bancak (left) and Doyok, with bull(?) and snakes above. Private collection (Cribb 1999, no. 218e).

Fig. 27 Drawing made for Raffles of zodiac beaker, East Java, 14th century. BM OA 1939.3-11.07(107), Raffles Collection.

Fig. 28 East Javanese bronze zodiac beakers collected by Raffles. One example (below left) is dated 1251 in the Shaka era (AD 1329). BM OA 1859.12-28.139 (left), 138 (centre) and 140 (right), Raffles Collection.

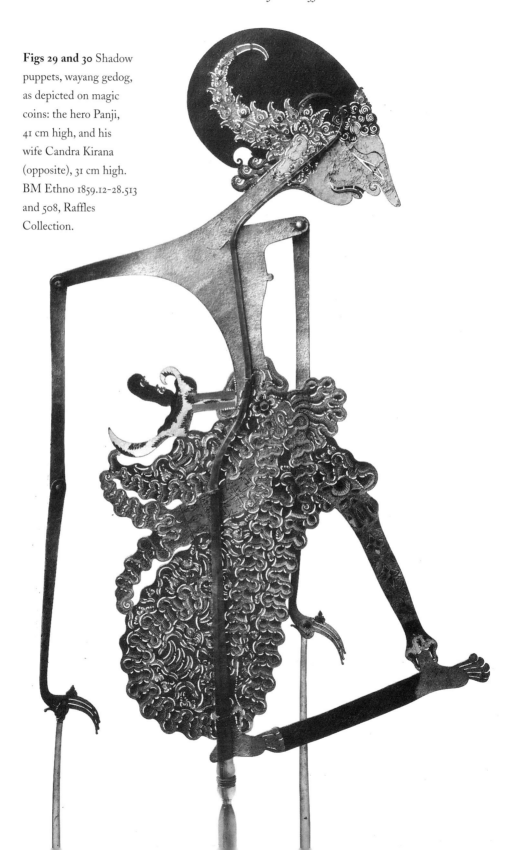

Figs 29 and 30 Shadow puppets, wayang gedog, as depicted on magic coins: the hero Panji, 41 cm high, and his wife Candra Kirana (opposite), 31 cm high. BM Ethno 1859.12-28.513 and 508, Raffles Collection.

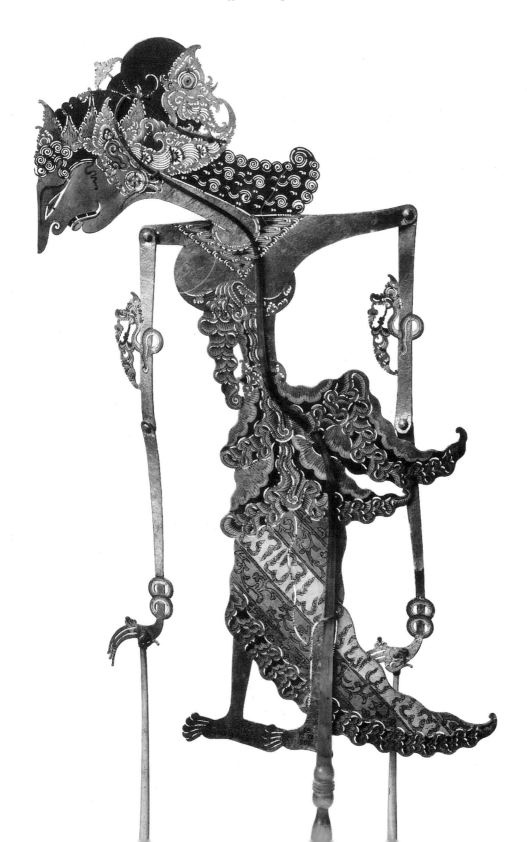

Figs 31 and 32 Shadow puppets, wayang gedog, as depicted on magic coins: Panji's servants Bancak (51 cm high) and (opposite) Doyok (31 cm high). Doyok is wearing a magic coin on a string round his neck. BM Ethno 1859.12-28.572 and 579, Raffles Collection.

Fig. 33 Drawing made for Raffles of a Majapahit period sculptural relief at Candi Sukuh in East Java, mid-15th century, of a servant figure, with features of Panji's servant Bancak. BM OA 1939.3-11.07(98).

THE RAFFLES GAMELANS

TIM BYARD-JONES

Imagine walking into one of the open-sided pavilions forming part of a Javanese royal palace. The roof is held up by ornately carved pillars and there is a raised, paved floor, but otherwise the building is open to the courtyard around it. On one side of the pavilion sits the Sultan, in his full regalia, surrounded by guards and courtiers. Along the side is an array of musical instruments unlike anything you have ever seen before. A group of perhaps thirty musicians are sitting cross-legged in front of the instruments. They have no conductor and no notation, yet they are producing a sonorous and totally ordered sound, using a scale which – if again not quite like anything you have ever heard before – is pleasing to the ear. This was what confronted Raffles on his visits to the palaces of Central Java in 1812. He had more pressing concerns on his mind at the time (principally the question of whether or not he was about to be murdered), but even so the music caught his interest sufficiently for him both to write sympathetically about it and to bring back to England at least two sets of instruments. Like so much else that Raffles brought back from Java, these sets of instruments (the word *gamelan* refers collectively to the set) constitute a vital resource in our understanding of the historical development of Javanese culture.

Basically, a Central Javanese classical gamelan consists of three sections: *balungan* or core melody instruments; punctuating instruments; and elaborating instruments, with control provided by the drums (there is no conductor in gamelan music). The melody section of a gamelan may include metallophones with bronze bars covering a range just over one octave, known as *demung* or *saron* (colour plate 6), with the latter sounding an octave higher than the former, and in addition one or more multi-octave metallophones known as *gambang gangsa*. Most modern gamelans still use demungs and sarons but have dispensed with the gambang gangsa in favour of a further one-octave metallophone sounding an octave higher than the saron. This section of instruments plays the core melody of the piece of music, or sometimes simple variations around the basic melody.

The punctuating instruments consist of various sizes of bronze gongs (hanging vertically from a stand) and gong kettles (resting horizontally on cords stretched across a frame). Three of these are represented in the Raffles gamelans: the gongs themselves, the *kenong* and the *kethuk*. One development which took place in the nineteenth century was a proliferation of the kenongs to cover every note in the scale. Also present in the Raffles gamelans is the *kecer* – a double pair of bronze cymbals, two resting on the wooden frame and the other two being held by the player. Though not always used in modern gamelan, they appear to have been an indispensable part of the gamelans of the early nineteenth century: several sets and pairs of cymbals are to be found among the items of The Raffles Collection (figs 34 and 35).

The elaborating instruments represented in the Raffles gamelans are the *bonang*, the *gender* and the *rebab*. The bonang is a gong chime consisting of ten small gong kettles, played with a beater in each hand, and is the leading instrument in 'loud' style pieces. The gender is a soft metallophone, played with a soft beater in each hand, while the rebab is a bowed fiddle of Arabic origin. The drums, known as *kendhang*, come in various sizes but are all basically of the same form: barrel shaped but slightly asymmetrical, one end larger than the other, with skins on both ends laced together round the outside, and played with the hands rather than sticks.

The origins of Javanese gamelan go back ultimately to the pre-Hindu period, and are possibly related to the Dongson bronze drum cultures found in mainland Southeast Asia. Javanese legend has the first gamelan – Lokananta – being forged by the gods in AD 230. Gong-shaped stones dating to a very early period have been found by archaeologists working in Central Java, and there are references to the playing of gamelan instruments in many of the medieval Javanese chronicles. As with other aspects of Javanese performing arts, it is impossible to reconstruct details of early performances from the literary evidence, and not until the eighteenth century do we start to find interpretable references.

In the gamelan, what survives of the pre-Islamic period are the gongs and kendhang-type drums. The two sacred pre-Islamic gamelan types of the Central Javanese courts (Munggangan and Kodhok Ngorek, still to be found today in the palaces of Yogyakarta and Surakarta) are formed almost exclusively of gongs, gong kettles and drums, as are animist 'folk' ensembles such as the Reog and Jatilan.

The coming of Islam in the fourteenth century brought about major changes in

Javanese culture. This is particularly marked in the northern coastal Pasisir region, where to this day a more orthodox form of Islam is practised than in the area around the Central Javanese court cities of Yogyakarta and Surakarta. The development of the Sekaten gamelan (still associated today with the celebrations of the Prophet Muhammad's birthday) is ascribed to Sunan Kalijaga (one of the *wali sanga*, the nine Islamic saints credited with the conversion of Java) in a literary work called the *Titi Asri*, which may or may not be an accurate historical record. In any case, it is this phase of gamelan development which saw the adoption of a section of sarons alongside gongs and bonangs. The only drum in a Sekaten gamelan is the *bedhug*, otherwise used in mosques to call the faithful to prayer: in contrast to the kendhang-type drums, the bedhug is symmetrical and the heads are nailed in place and played with a stick.

The Hindu Javanese who refused to convert to Islam mostly fled to Bali, which remains Hindu to this day. Balinese culture appears to have preserved a number of features which were probably the norm in Java too until comparatively recent times. Among these are the use of genders to accompany the *wayang kulit* shadow-puppet plays, which are not otherwise integrated into the gamelan ensemble, and the use of the bamboo *calung* as a domestic instrument.

It was probably only in the eighteenth century that 'soft' instruments (gender, gambang, rebab and suling) were added to the gamelan. By the end of the eighteenth century, the instrumentation had settled down into the sections – if not the exact instrumentation – that we find today, though more instruments would be added and duplicated during the nineteenth and early twentieth centuries.

The gender in Java still has a special role in the accompaniment of wayang, which until recently was provided by a special gamelan wayang rather than a full ensemble. The use of the gambang as a domestic instrument for solitary playing is attested by the fact that when Professor Crotch transcribed the playing of Raden Rana Dipura (who had accompanied Raffles to England) it was the gambang that Rana Dipura chose to play to him, although other instruments were available.

Of the other 'soft' instruments in the modern gamelan, the *suling* (a bamboo flute) is presumed to be a folk instrument of great antiquity, though owing to the perishable nature of bamboo, archaeological evidence for this is sadly lacking. The rebab is undeniably of Arabic provenance, placing its entry into the gamelan firmly into the Islamic period, but the gender *panerus* may be only a century or so old, having been invented to provide the gender with a 'baby sibling' analogous to the bonang panerus and the saron panerus. Most surprising of all, the modern style of women's singing – *sindhenan* – was only invented around the time of the First World War, though it has quickly achieved dominance of the gamelan soundscape, particularly since amplification has been available.

Raffles brought back to England two full-sized and one model gamelan. The model is significant because it is the one depicted in the engraving of a gamelan in *The History of Java* (fig. 35). Together with the full-sized gamelans, one now in the British Museum (fig. 34) and the other at Claydon House in Buckinghamshire, it provides important evidence as to the instrumentation and tuning of gamelans used at the beginning of the nineteenth century. Then, as now, two tuning systems were used in gamelan: the five-note *slendro* and the seven-note *pelog*. All the Raffles instruments were originally in the slendro tuning, and the model, too – judging from the number of notes on the various instruments – represents a slendro set.

The carving on the frames of both full-sized gamelans is particularly fine, and is easily up to Central Javanese court standards. The frames of the British Museum set are unique: nothing remotely like them survives in any other known gamelan, whether in Java or elsewhere. The instruments are all highly zoomorphic, with frames carved to represent peacocks, dragons, deer and so forth (colour plate 6). The gong stand is surmounted by an eagle, which gives a possible clue to the origin of this set of instruments, since a Javanese document of around 1800 from Gresik in East Java (just north of Surabaya) illustrates a slendro gamelan with just such a gong stand. Gresik appears to have been a major centre of gamelan manufacture around this period (the Claydon House instruments originally belonged to the Dutch Resident of Gresik and were made around 1780), so Gresik could also be the source of the British Museum set.

Unfortunately, some degree of scrambling between the two sets took place after their arrival in England, so that notes originally belonging to the Claydon House instruments can be found on the British Museum set, and vice versa. There are identifying marks on the frames and bars of the Claydon House sarons, which also show signs of the filing and scraping which is done when a gamelan is tuned. The identifying marks are undoubtedly Javanese in origin: similar marks can be found on many other gamelans. Evidence of tuning is also significant because a newly forged gamelan is rather unstable in its tuning: most Javanese gamelan makers expect a new bronze gamelan to be tuned after one, two, five and ten years, after which tuning is only required to repair accidental damage. This would imply that the Claydon House instruments had been used, while the British Museum set may have been specially made for Raffles and may not have been played for long – if at all – before being shipped to England.

Unfortunately, while the Raffles instruments give us a fairly clear picture of the instrumentation of gamelans around the turn of the nineteenth century, we are on less certain ground when it comes to the music that would have been played on them: notation systems were only devised in the Javanese palaces at the very end of the nineteenth century, while the system most commonly used today was developed in the early twentieth century. Here too Raffles provides modern gamelan scholars with important evidence: his description of gamelan in *The History of Java* is one of the first helpful accounts we have, in sharp contrast to earlier books such as Stockdale's *The Island of Java* (1811), which mentions only '... a certain kind of musical instruments, called *gomgoms*, consisting of hollow iron bowls, of various sizes and tones, upon which a man strikes with an iron or wooden stick; their harmony is not disagreeable, and they are not unlike a set of bells', a reference which is completely useless to modern scholars. In contrast, Raffles described performances, gave accurate names for instruments and even included a glossary of musical terms in Javanese. The transcriptions of Javanese pieces are likewise among the earliest of Javanese music.

The century after the publication of *The History of Java* was to see an awakening of European interest in and appreciation of non-Western music. The French composer Debussy, for example, on first hearing a gamelan play in 1889, was moved to remark that, in comparison, European percussion was '... like noises at a country fair'. Since then, many Westerners have been lured to Java by the gamelan to study and research its music, and many more play gamelan in their own countries. For instance, Britain now has about fifty active gamelan groups, while in the US there are well over a hundred. All of us now involved in gamelan must acknowledge the pioneering work done by Raffles in bringing gamelan to Europe and in taking such an open-minded interest in Javanese music.

Fig. 34 Engraving from *The Illustrated London News*, 12 May 1860, captioned 'Javanese musical instruments recently added to the British Museum'. It shows the Raffles gamelan together with Thai and other musical instruments given to the Museum at the same time.

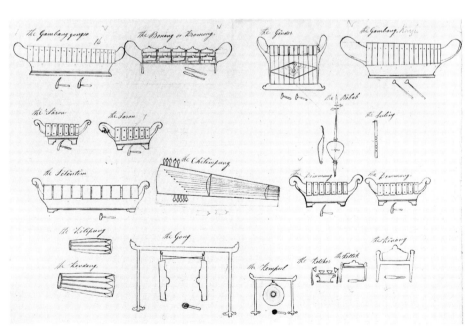

Fig. 35 Pen-and-ink drawing used as the basis for an engraving of a gamelan in Raffles's *History of Java*. BM OA 1939.3-11.09(15), Raffles Collection.

Claiming the High Ground: Tengger Buddhism

JEFF ROBERTS

In the summer of 1815, Thomas Stamford Raffles, Lieutenant-Governor of Java during the British Interregnum (1811-16), made an extensive tour of his island domain. Among his papers lodged in the Department of Oriental Antiquities in the British Museum is a sketch map of the area (fig. 36). Officially, the reason for this trip seems to have been to assess the impact of the land-revenue system that he had introduced the year before. Whenever possible, however, Raffles also found time to further his own personal study of Javanese culture and society. It was this scholarly interest that, on 7 June, appears to have drawn him to the Tengger highlands, a relatively isolated volcanic massif in the east of the island.

Raffles was by no means the first European visitor to these mountains. There are reports of Dutch soldiers in the highlands, in pursuit of native rebels, as early as the 1670s, only fifty or so years after the Netherlands East Indies Company (Vereenigde Ostindische Compagnie, hereafter VOC) had gained a foothold on Java. They were to return at fairly regular intervals, destroying the odd village in the process, until the entire region eventually came under Dutch control in 1764.

Nor was Raffles the first European to take an interest in this region. The earliest published mention of the highlands in a European language seems to have appeared in the letters pages of the *Bataviasche Courant* of 1785. There, Jan Hooijman, a Dutch merchant based in Batavia (now Jakarta), had written requesting verification of a report that 'a sort of a people' (*een soort van volk*) had recently sacrificed a human victim to the crater of Mount Bromo, an active volcano high in the middle of the Tengger massif. Adriaan van Rijck, the VOC's Kommandant at nearby Pasuruan, replied that, though there may have been some precedent for this report, such practices were no longer known in the region. While they might have once been murderous pagans, according to van Rijck, the inhabitants of these mountains were now Muslims just like their lowland Javanese neighbours.

It was the religion of highland people that seems to have most interested Raffles. During his visit, he reported, he met and interviewed local priests, who though being 'in general intelligent men can produce no traditional history of their origin, whence they came, or who entrusted them with the sacred books, to the faith contained in which they still adhere'.[1] When questioned about that 'faith', however, they proved rather more forthcoming:

> They replied that they believed in a *dewa* [deity], who was all-powerful ... and that
> the particulars of their worship were contained in a book called *Panglawu*, which
> they presented to me.[2]

Later that year Raffles gave a lecture in Batavia in which he publicized his understanding of the contents of this 'book'. There and in his encyclopaedic *History of Java* he claimed that in Tengger he had found:

> ... the remnant of a people still following the Hindu worship ... the sole depositaries
> [sic] of the rites and doctrines of that religion existing at this day on Java.[3]

This report, at considerable odds with that of van Rijck, was to have a great influence on subsequent writings about the highlands. More importantly, perhaps, it would also have far-reaching consequences for the people who lived there.

The following year, 1816, Britain handed Java over to the Netherlands East Indies government, the bankrupt VOC having been dissolved in 1800. If there were many visitors to the highlands in the early years of this new phase of Dutch rule, then few seem to have written about their experiences. As Hageman suggests, most simply 'came, saw – and went. A cold nose was enough' (*De reizigers kwamen, – zagen, – en gingen. Een koude neus was genoeg*).[4] One exception was van Isseldijk, who, using the *nom de plume* 'Y', wrote about Tengger for the *Bataviasche Courant* of 1820. Agreeing with Raffles about local religion, he went on to warn that the region's Hindu 'remnants' were currently under threat from the large numbers of lowland Muslims moving into these still relatively under-populated mountains.

Twelve years later another visitor, Domis, not only concurred with this prognosis, but elaborated upon its dramatic theme. Whereas Raffles had claimed that highlanders could give no account of their origins, Domis seems to have elicited from them a number of suggestions. Some said that their forebears had come from Mataram, far to the west; others that they were from nearby Malang. Dismissing these claims as 'confused' (*verwarde*),[5] however, he formed his own opinion: that highlanders were the descendants of refugees from Majapahit, a Hindu-Buddhist kingdom in the nearby lowlands which had collapsed in the early sixteenth century, apparently under pressure from Islamic rivals. Over the next few decades, this image of highlanders as a besieged enclave of cultural throwbacks not only became a scholarly orthodoxy, but went on to influence colonial policy on native religion.

On defeating the neighbouring kingdom of Blambangan in the late eighteenth century, the VOC had forced its Hindu subjects to convert to Islam. In this way, they hoped to loosen ties between East Java and nearby Bali, whose Hindu rajas were proving hostile to the European presence in the region. Roughly a century later in Tengger, however, the Dutch opted for a rather different approach. Now they were less wary of Hindu Bali than of Islam, which had become a potentially dangerous focus for anti-Dutch sentiments. Influenced by what Raffles, Domis and others had written about highland people and their ways, the colonial government legislated to actively preserve these living 'remnants' of Hindu Java as a bulwark against Islam. While this strategy was far from successful in containing Islam in the Indies as a whole, locally it proved reasonably effective. To this day, the vast majority of villagers in the upper slopes of the highlands remain of a non-Islamic religious persuasion.

Yet, if it has long been fairly clear that highlanders are not Muslims, more recently the question of what religion they actually follow has proved rather more controversial. In late 1950s Indonesia, a number of Islamic intellectuals not only disputed the notion that highland people were Hindus, but argued that theirs was not a 'real' religion, but merely a collection of superstitious beliefs and customs. Since, according to the Indonesian constitution, all citizens are required to profess a recognized world religion, such claims were potentially rather damaging. For highlanders, they were also rather difficult to counter. Contemporary reports suggest that most Tengger villagers knew little or nothing of Hindu beliefs or even deities, but only of the ancestors and territorial spirits supplicated by their priests. To make matters even more difficult, they themselves called their religion, not Hindu, but Budha, a term which in Javanese can denote an array of traditional practices associated with the island's pre-Islamic past.

The remarks about Tengger tradition had been made in the course of a more sustained attack on Balinese Hinduism which, at the time, was not recognized as a legitimate religion by the Indonesian state. In Bali, however, such claims were countered by a number of Hindu organizations which had been actively promoting and developing Balinese religion for some years. Eventually, after much tense deliberation between these organizations and the Ministry of Religion, Hinduism was finally included in the list of five religions recognized by the Indonesian state (Islam, Catholicism, Protestantism, Buddhism and Hinduism), and Balinese were legally allowed to register themselves as Hindus. Meanwhile, the state made one particular Balinese organization, the Parisada Hindu Dharma (Hindu Dharma Council), responsible for representing Hindus, not just in Bali but throughout Indonesia.

Hearing of these developments, some highland leaders sought a similar solution to their difficulties with officialdom. Citing a number of similarities between Tengger religious practices and those of the Balinese, a number of priests and village headmen argued that they too were Hindus. During the 1970s, increasing numbers of highlanders began to follow the Balinese example and register themselves as Hindus. Guided by representatives of the Parisada Hindu Dharma, they also began an ongoing 'reform' of their traditional religious practices, bringing them increasingly into line with the norms of Hindu worship as known in Bali.

Nearly two centuries after Raffles first proposed the notion, then, it would seem that one might now say, with some degree of certainty, that Tengger highlanders are Hindus. Moreover, it is as Hindus, the exotic remnants of the once great Majapahit, that they have come to be represented to the world at large. In recent years thousands of foreign tourist have visited the region, attracted by the films, guidebooks and other productions of the Indonesian 'heritage industry' in which such images have pride of place.

As for the 'book' on which Raffles had originally based his opinions, ideas about the contents of this continue to play an important part in debates about highland religion. While Raffles indicated, in a footnote to *The History of Java*, that he intended to publish at least part of its contents, it appears that he never actually did so. Recently, however, Nancy Smith-Hefner, an American scholar who has been working in and on the Tengger region since the 1970s, has suggested that Raffles had copies made and that one currently sits in the British Library. The manuscript concerned, MS Add. 123424 – a collection of *mantra* written in Javanese script on Javanese paper, with a note in English on its fly-leaf, 'Sacred book of the Hindoo of the Mountain of Tangar'[6] – would certainly seem to fit the bill. Moreover, Smith-Hefner's analysis of its contents suggests an even closer fit. After transcribing the *mantra*, she compared them with two other texts that she had collected during the 1980s in the highlands where, known as the *Purwa Bumi* (Origin of the World) they were still used in purification rites by Tengger priests. From her analysis she concludes that these latter texts are 'the same' as that collected by Raffles.[7]

Alongside these three sets of *mantra*, however, she presents a fourth, a version of a text also used for purificatory rites but in Bali.[8] As this also closely resembles those from Tengger, Smith-Hefner suggests that there must have been historical links between the traditions from which all four texts derived. More generally, she concludes that Tengger and Balinese religion originated from one source, the Hindu-Buddhist kingdom of Majapahit. The British Library manuscript, then, would seem not only to confirm Raffles's opinion about the nature of highland religion, but also to provide documentary evidence for Domis's later hypothesis about its historical origin.

As Smith-Hefner herself points out, however, the relation between this manuscript and Raffles's 'book' is not exactly clear. According to the British Library's records, MS Add. 123424 was purchased in 1842, not from Raffles or his estate, but from John Crawfurd Esq., one-time British Resident at the Javanese court of Yogyakarta and, like Raffles, a keen collector of Javanese manuscripts. Indeed, both the name that Raffles attached to his 'book', *Panglawu*, and the brief extracts from Tengger liturgy that he cited in *The History of Java* suggest other *mantra*, also still in use in the highlands, but different to the *Purwa Bumi* considered by Smith-Hefner. While none of this disqualifies the British Library manuscript from being a copy of Raffles's 'book', it does raise the possibility that there was more than one set of Tengger *mantra* in circulation among nineteenth-century British Javanophiles. Yet, whatever its pedigree, judging by this manuscript it would seem that there has been remarkably little change in the liturgy of highland priests over the past two centuries.

Smith-Hefner's more ambitious conclusions as to how the *Purwa Bumi* came to be a part of Tengger tradition are also open to question. On the evidence of the British Library manuscript, it would seem fairly clear that this *mantra* was known in the highlands in the early nineteenth century. As to its prior history, however, it is difficult to establish much at all. While Smith-Hefner's suggestion that it arrived there from

Majapahit is highly plausible, it is by no means the only possibility. Why, for instance, might it not have come from Bali? After all, Balinese rajas are reported to have visited Tengger in the late seventeenth century,[9] to worship at a shrine near Mount Semeru, the tallest mountain in the highlands and, indeed, in Java as a whole. There, it seems one of the rajas was given a *kris* (dagger) by a local priest. Perhaps, then, the Balinese had brought the *mantra* with them and had given it in exchange to the Tengger priest. In speculating this way, however, my purpose is not to proffer an alternative to Smith-Hefner's theory about the provenance of this fascinating text. Rather, I merely wish to set the scene for a more recent episode in its entangled story; an episode which, I suggest, invites us to imagine Tengger highlanders less as anachronistic remnants of pre-Islamic Java than as the creative practitioners of a living tradition.

In 1993, I also began research in the Tengger highlands. What drew me to the region, however, was not a question of whether the residents were really Hindus or not; neither did I hope to discover their ancestral origins. Rather, I was most interested in what contemporary highlanders had to say about the events of the recent past, events in which such questions and, perhaps more importantly, other people's answers to them, had seemed to play an important role. The village where I lived for a year and a half, in the southwest of the highlands, proved to be an interesting site from which to explore such issues. There, despite the large and expert body of opinion to the contrary, people rejected the notion that they were or ever had been Hindus. Neither were they Muslims. Rather, while recognizing that their religious tradition shared something with those of their neighbours, they seemed most concerned to maintain its unique local character. Retaining the older name of Budha for this tradition, they had for some years actively resisted the reforms taking place in other highland villages.

On the whole, highland people are extremely sociable and obligingly talkative on any number of themes. Perhaps unsurprisingly, though, whenever I asked about religion in this Budha village, people seemed reluctant to say much at all. Often they denied that they were qualified to talk about such things and suggested that I had better ask the village priest. With him, however, unlike my illustrious forebear Raffles, I came up against a further wall of polite but firm secrecy.

Eventually, though, after several frustrating months, I became friendly with a man who was not only prepared to consider my questions, but showed me several exercise books filled with handwritten copies of *mantra*. This, he claimed with some pride, was the most complete collection of authentic Tengger *mantra* in existence, unlike those used in the Hindu villages to the north. After studying these texts for a while, I found that the *Purwa Bumi*, mentioned above, was not among them. Given its apparently Hindu associations, I wondered whether it was no longer being used in this village or if perhaps it was being withheld from me. My friend, however, claimed that, while he had heard of the *Purwa Bumi*, he was unaware if it was used anywhere in the highlands. Maybe, he suggested, I would come across it in one of the Hindu villages. If I did, he asked, could I try to get a copy for his collection?

Gradually, my social networks became wider and more fruitful. I met many people all over the highlands who, in the privacy of their own homes, positively delighted in discussing local ways and their history. From some of these I learned *mantra* which they used for a wide range of purposes, from healing and protecting themselves and their families to farming and even finding lost property. Like the others that I had already studied, these *mantra* were peppered with references to Hindu deities, as well as the more 'indigenous' spirit-guardians of the island of Java. Alongside them, however, there were a number of unmistakably Arabic words and phrases. When I mentioned this, my teachers generally dismissed the suggestion of an Islamic influence. One man, a self-proclaimed Hindu, said emphatically that it did not matter where these words came from. What was important, he added, was that they were proven to be powerful and that one dared to use them.

As he and his companions went on to elaborate upon this notion, I began to get a very strong sense of Tengger tradition as radically eclectic in character. Rather than being essentially of this or that particular religion, categories that had, after all, been defined elsewhere, I wondered if highlanders had not been actively and experimentally borrowing from the array of influences that had come their way over hundreds of years. It would, of course, be difficult to provide historical evidence for such an impression or, for that matter, even conceive of what it might consist. As a way of understanding how highlanders continued to make sense of their own rich past, however, it proved extremely revealing.

Towards the end of my stay I spent an evening in a Hindu village in the northeast, discussing Tengger liturgy with two priests, one of whom was acknowledged as the 'head' of the whole region. To my surprise, these men told me that they too knew nothing of the *Purwa Bumi* except its name. Even more surprisingly, however, one added that he had heard that there was a manuscript containing this *mantra* in a museum in 'Holland', the name which, like many other rural Javanese, highlanders often give to anywhere overseas. He claimed to have read of it in a book written by an Indonesian anthropologist who had been working in the region a few years previously. The other priest said that he too had read something similar in a book written in Indonesian by Bu Nengsi (Mrs/Mother Nancy), as Smith-Hefner is known to many highland people. Both men asked if I knew of this manuscript and if I could get them a copy. One even offered to let me consult his collection of *mantra* in exchange. As I had a photocopy of Smith-Hefner's article with the multiple versions of the *Purwa Bumi* back in my home village, I agreed to make copies in a nearby town and bring them on my next visit.

A few weeks later, I returned to the northeast to say my farewells before leaving for London. When I delivered the photocopy to the house of the one priest, I found him alone at his fireside, giving us a rare opportunity to talk in private. He examined the document for a long time, muttering and making exclamations of pleasant surprise at regular intervals, occasionally asking me to clarify which of the different versions was which. Later, as agreed, he brought out his books of *mantra* for me to see. Looking them over I saw that, as he had suggested at our earlier meeting, the *Purwa Bumi* was not among them. When I asked what he would do with this *mantra* now that he had it, the priest shrugged. While he was very grateful that I had brought it, he said that he could not be sure if any of the versions really was the *Purwa Bumi*. Moreover, as this *mantra* had not been known in his village for a long time, he did not know how it should be used. Maybe the *Purwa Bumi* did not really belong there anyway. In short, at present he could not tell. He would consult the head priest in due course and suggested that, if I wanted to know more, I do the same. Unfortunately, however, though I delivered the photocopy to the head priest's house as promised, I never had an opportunity to talk to him again before I left Java.

While I cannot tell exactly what would be made of the *Purwa Bumi*, the reception it received was not at all the dramatic homecoming of a lost cultural treasure that one might have expected. The priest with whom I spoke seemed hesitant and above all cautious about the prospect of working this new arrival into Tengger tradition. The *Purwa Bumi*, like all *mantra*, was composed of powerful words, and using them involved taking responsibility for the consequences. As the spiritual representative of a whole village, then, this was not something that the priest could afford to take lightly. On the other hand, as an aficionado of local lore, his pleasure at having and being able to study this text was obvious. Either way, he seemed to view the *mantra* less as a symbol of regional heritage, a reminder of the dead and distant past, than as something with an unknown potential for the future.

Before leaving the highlands altogether, I also gave a copy of the *Purwa Bumi* to the friend who had first asked for one back in the Budha village. Delighted to receive it, especially when I told him of Raffles and the circuitous route it had taken, he duly added the photocopy to his collection of authentic Tengger *mantra*. When I asked what he would do with it, he replied that he would simply keep it safe for future generations. Who knows, he said, perhaps they would find a use for it.

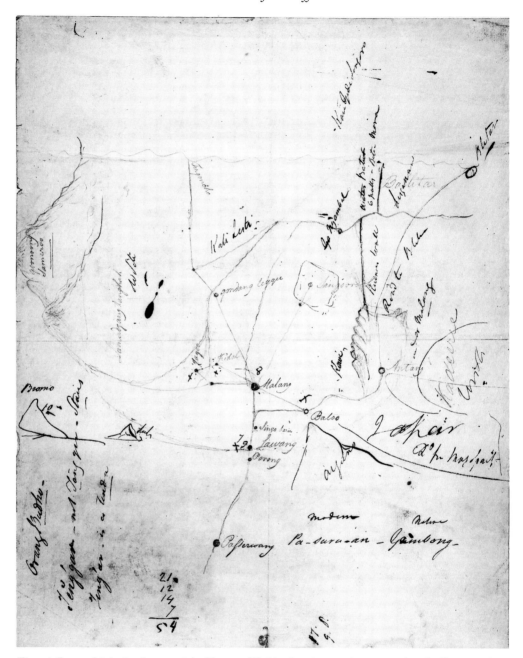

Fig. 36 Pen-and-ink sketch map of the Tengger Highland region, made in 1815 when Raffles visited the area. BM OA 1939.3-11.09(7), Raffles Collection.

White Elephants
and Cannibals

Nigel Barley

When Sir Stamford Raffles returned to London in 1816, he brought with him not just material we would now call Indonesian. There was also a sizeable Japanese collection. An entry in the Treasury minute book lists his goods as including '3 cases containing Specimens of Japanese Costumes and Manufactures – Crapes and Silks – 12 Cups of peculiar manufacture of Porcelaine,' and later 'some trifling Articles of prohibited Japan manufacture'.[1]

The only material of this kind that survived to come to the British Museum was two curious wooden masks, possibly used in Shinto ritual drama (figs 38 and 39).

This lost collection was the result of a commercial expedition that Raffles had planned since 1811 when compiling intelligence reports for Lord Minto (Governor-General of India) in preparation for the British invasion of Java. Raffles had a high regard for the Japanese. In his address to the Batavian Society of Arts and Sciences in 1815 he accorded them the highest possible compliment:

> They are represented to be a nervous, vigorous people, whose bodily and mental
> powers assimilate much nearer to those of Europe, than what is attributed to Asiatics
> in general. Their features are masculine and perfectly European.[2]

Echoing Sir William Jones, he noted that Japan bore 'a pre-eminence among Eastern kingdoms, analogous to that of Britain among the nations of the West'.[3] Not just quasi-Westerners, the Japanese were almost British.

At that time, the Dutch were the only Western power permitted to trade with Japan through the small offshore island of Deshima near Nagasaki. Raffles argued that this trading factory was a dependency of Java and that, since he had assumed control of Java, he had assumed control of Deshima. In 1813, he despatched two ships, the *Charlotte* and

Mary to open trade under the command of a Dutch trader and an allegedly alcoholic Scots surgeon. Lest the Japanese show hostility to the British, the crew were to pretend to be Americans.

Not surprisingly, matters became complicated. The Dutch showed themselves ill-disposed to accepting Raffles's authority and raising the Union Jack. The Japanese set their faces against officially quite knowing what was going on. Finally, after multiple prevarications, trade was opened and a return cargo secured. In the following year, a second cargo was sent. The accounts, with all their presents, duties, commissions, currencies and previous debts, were hugely complicated and Raffles managed to present them as showing a handsome profit. His enemies in Calcutta would later rejig them to show a loss and poison the Governor General's mind against him so that the trade was allowed to lapse. One of the enduring traits of the founder of Singapore was that he was a disastrous businessman. At least he would get material out of the mission for his paper given to the Batavian Society of Arts and Sciences.

The nature of the cargoes is interesting. The principal commodities from Java were sugar, spices, tin, woollen goods and Indian cloths. The woollen goods were a particular concern of Raffles as constituting the basis of a possible trade between Britain and Japan. The tin was an old obsession, dating from an intelligence report of 1810 noting the tin mines of Banca that Raffles promptly seized following the British takeover. Raffles was doggedly convinced he would be able to turn them to profit or use them as the basis for a tin currency. Dr Thomas Horsfield, Raffles's principal man of science (fig. 6), was depatched to conduct a survey. The mines, however, proved a considerable and tiresome financial drain that Raffles explained away as due to 'unexpected difficulties and disappointments'.[4]

The return cargo would be in Japanese copper, camphor and pitch. But the most revealing element buried in all the documentation is the presents for the various officials and the Japanese shogun.[5]

There are the usual scientific and surgical instruments, telescopes and looking-glasses, and practical gifts of paper and pencils for the interpreters. Notable, however, is the range of presents of botanical and zoological interest. There are plants and seeds, a botanical dictionary, natural history drawings, live birds, sheep and civet cats. Raffles's personal, scholarly interests seem to be intruding here, as usual, on trade and even gaining the upper hand. But the prize object was a five-year-old Ceylon elephant intended for the shogun. (Throughout the documentation there is reflected the great confusion in the minds of Westerners between the Emperor and the shogun, but it seems clear that the present was indeed intended for the shogun who was, at that time, the effective ruler.)

The female elephant clearly caused a stir, inducing something of a frenzy among the artists of Nagasaki. Many images of it survive (colour plate 7). It seems to have been despatched via Batavia but accompanied by its mahoud, who is shown in several of the pictures. The technology of elephant-handling seems also to have exercised some fascination and there are drawings of the implements used to control and feed the beast. One of the most complex images is that bound into a book, ex-Siebold collection, in the British Library (Or. 913) with glued-on flaps that can be raised to show different bodily parts in different postures. A note is attached, detailing traditional court usages involving elephants in China. Other animals from the Raffles expedition are shown in the same book.

The primordial importance of imported foreign animals for the development of natural history in Japan has been recognized in a recent publication and exhibition at the Suntory Museum in Tokyo, *Nihon hakubutsu-gabu kotohajime – egakareta shizen* ('The beginning of natural history study in Japan – the natural world as depicted by artists'), providing as they did a stimulus for close inquiry and observation. So Raffles may unwittingly have succeeded at least as much in Japan as in Great Britain in his efforts to further the discipline of natural history.

The elephant, in more immediate terms, might be counted rather less of a success. It seems that, for once, Raffles was short of exactly the sort of nuts-and-bolts information on which he normally prided himself. The Japanese authorities, suspicious of Western intentions, did not permit the construction of deep-water jetties but obliged traders to transship their goods into small boats under the guns of the fort. While an elephant can swim, it cannot dive. It seems to have proved impossible to unload the beast at all, although the shogun graciously sent a hundred bales of wheat for its maintenance on the return journey back to Batavia, where it disappears from history.

One other element of the cargo is of interest. Included, apparently partly as a commodity for sale and partly as a gift for the shogun and the interpreters, are fifty pounds of Egyptian mummy. Egyptian mummies had a peculiar place in the Western world in the eighteenth and early nineteenth century. Large numbers of Egyptian mummies, both animal and human, were excavated and ground up for sale. Human mummies were the most prized and Raffles repeatedly stresses that all the goods for

Japan must be of the highest quality only. Mummies were an important source of pigment for oil paints, giving a deep brown shade not attainable by any other means. But minced 'mummy' was also an important drug and used as a panacaea, to the point where an industry producing fake mummy from the corpses of executed felons prospered to supply the demand from the apothecaries' trade.

There is an irony in this attempt to encourage the consumption of human remains by the civilized shogun of Japan. In many ways Stamford Raffles was more a man of the eighteenth than the nineteenth century. Despite his firm universalist humanism he had strong evolutionist assumptions, but his was the evolutionism of Lamarck rather than Darwin: he believed that acquired characteristics – adaptations to the environment and expressions of wants – could be passed on directly to offspring. This view perhaps encouraged two aspects of his vision of humanity: first, Man's potential perfectability through social means, and second, the possibility of the arrangement of societies on an evolutionary scale, running from savagery to civilization. This view informed his political philosophy as well as his natural history. His exposure to more 'barbaric' Bengkulu after 'civilized' Java led to a determination to adopt a more interventionist policy, which he justified most clearly in a letter to Thomas Murdoch in 1820:

> There appear to be certain stages and gradations through which society must run its course to civilization, and which can no more be overleaped or omitted, than men can arrive at maturity without passing through the gradations of infancy and youth. Independence is the characteristic of the savage state; but while men continue disinterested, and with little mutual dependence on each other, they can never become civilized.

He followed this with a typically Rafflesian jibe at himself: 'Tyrants seldom want an excuse and in becoming a despot I am anxious to give you mine.'[6]

Cannibalism was for Raffles a particularly clear marker of savagery, just as architecture, writing and astronomy were signs of civilization. He therefore felt a sense of mental and moral outrage when he discovered that the Batak of north Sumatra practised all these arts of civilization alongside cannibalism. Significantly, his collection seems to have contained both a Batak bone writing-tablet and a diviner's staff (fig. 37).

In 1820, Raffles had just founded the colony of Singapore in the teeth of explicit instructions to the contrary from London. There was a very real possibility that the Dutch, who objected to the establishment, would invade. The signing of the peace treaties to end the Napoleonic Wars all over Europe was being held up. Raffles had every expectation of dismissal. He had suffered a prolonged absence from his beloved wife and children in Calcutta and undergone one of the periodic bouts of extreme illness that were the first symptoms of the brain tumour that would soon kill him. It might be expected that he would make all speed to return home to Bengkulu. In fact, his one thought was to divert his ship into Tapanuli harbour so that he might conduct fieldwork on the subject of cannibalism among the local Batak.

He sent a deliberately lurid account of these researches to his friend, the Duchess of Somerset, who had provided temporary housing in London for part of what is now known as The Raffles Collection – 'I am forming a collection of skulls, some from Battas that have been eaten. Will your Grace allow them room among the curiosities?' and a more factually detailed version for Thomas Marsden, the natural historian and geographer.

Anthropologists have long been interested in the Batak as one of the prime exponents of asymmetric cross-cousin marriage, i.e. a system of marital exchange that divides the social world into groups that are exclusively givers or takers of wives. Raffles's fieldwork was sufficiently detailed to pick up this concern with exchange and being eaten as a punishment for the sexual consumption of forbidden flesh. But his account of his enquiries shows that he was most astonished to find that people were eaten not in mad passion but in a quiet, orderly, rule-following way. This seems to have offered a way out of the contradiction and, ignoring part of his own evidence, he interprets cannibalism as simply an extreme form of capital punishment of strong deterrent effect:

> The Battas [Batak] have many virtues. I prize them highly. However horrible eating
> a man may sound in European ears, I question whether the party suffers so much, or
> the punishment itself is worse than the European tortures of two centuries ago. I have
> always doubted the policy, and even the right of capital punishment among civilized
> nations; but this once admitted, and torture allowed, I see nothing more cruel in
> eating a man alive than in torturing him for days with mangled limbs and the like.

He concluded:

The Battas are honest and honourable, and possess many more virtues than I have time to put down. ... I have arranged to pay a visit to Tobah and the banks of the great lake, in the course of the next year, and my plan is to go into the interior by way of Barus and return by way of Natal ... Lady Raffles will, I hope, accompany me and I shall endeavour to give up a full six weeks for the trip. I am perfectly satisfied that we shall be safe and I hardly know any people on whom I would sooner rely than the Battas.[7]

That fieldwork never took place, but Raffles did encourage the missionary Richard Burton to write an account of the Batak under the protection of the same British post at Tapanuli. As for cannibalism, the subject maintained its fascination for him. When Raffles lived in retirement in Hendon his neighbour was William Wilberforce, the abolitionist. On 28 March 1825, Wilberforce noted in his diary:

Sir Stamford and Lady Raffles and Dr. Morrison, the Chinese scholar, came between one and two – Lord Gombier called and we had an entertaining confabulation ... Singular criminal law of Batas by which persons committing great crimes sentenced to be eat up alive, the injured party having the first choice, the ear claimed and eat etc., until the mass fall on. The coup de grace, except in strong cases, given early. When Sir Stamford contended against the practice, the people urged, 'What defence can we have for our morals?'.[8]

Batak cannibalism is therefore not savage cannibalism at all, but deeply embedded in morality. Raffles's classification of the world is saved. Perhaps this is the background that sheds light on another entry in those same Treasury lists that show Raffles's lost Japanese collection in 1816. It mentions enigmatically 'three small mummies' shipped back from Java. Did Raffles himself eat mummy in defiance of his own notions of the place of cannibalism? But perhaps, like Batak cannibalism, eating mummy was not *really* cannibalism. It was just taking medicine, so the civilized – almost British – shogun of Japan could be encouraged to do it too.

Fig. 37 Detail of a carved wooden staff belonging to Raffles, made by the Batak people of Sumatra, 18th or 19th century. Usually owned by priests, such objects were considered the source of their divine power and often depict a legend in which incestuous boy-and-girl twin ancestors are absorbed into a tree trunk. BM Ethno As 1939.04.109, Raffles Collection, presented by Mrs J. Drake.

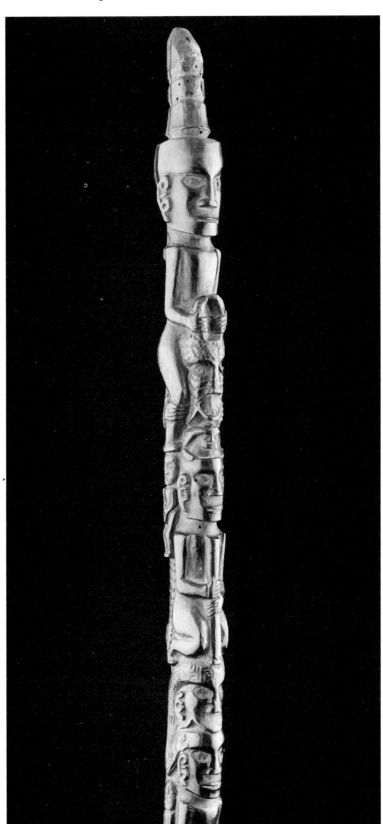

Figs 38 and 39 Two 19th-century painted wooden masks, probably from a Shinto ritual drama, from Japan. JA 1859.12-28.299 and 300, Raffles Collection.

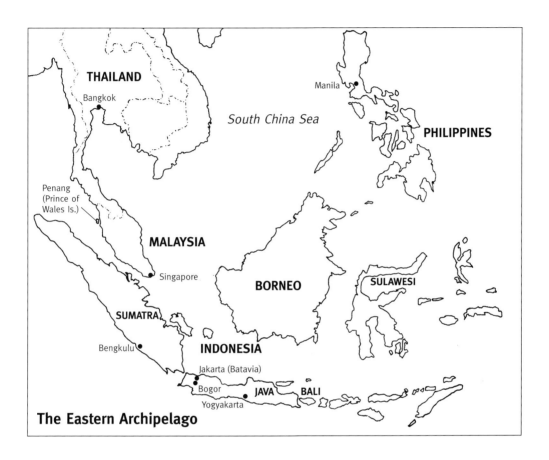

THAILAND

Bangkok

South China Sea

Manila

PHILIPPINES

Penang
(Prince of
Wales Is.)

MALAYSIA

Singapore

SUMATRA

BORNEO

SULAWESI

Bengkulu

INDONESIA

Jakarta (Batavia)

Bogor

JAVA

BALI

Yogyakarta

The Eastern Archipelago

NOTES

INTRODUCTION

1 Some possible Raffles material, such as armour from Borneo, given by the Venerable S.R. Raffles Flint, is still in the Royal Cornwall Museum.

2 It is clear that material was also sent back piecemeal, e.g. the Nias material which was probably not acquired until 1820, when Raffles briefly assumed sovereignty over Nias.

3 Scott-Kemball, n.d., p. 10.

4 Wurtzburg, 1968, p. 687.

5 Raffles, 1817: Appendix E, p. clvi.

BATIK: THE CLOTH OF KINGS

1 Raffles, 1817, p. 169.

2 Lady Raffles, 1830, p. 194.

3 Forge, 1989, p. 91.

4 Djoemena, 1993, p. 434.

5 BM Ethno As 1939.04.119 and 120, Raffles Collection.

6 Lady Raffles, 1830, p. 186.

7 Lady Raffles, 1830, p. 186.

8 Carey, 1992, p. 503.

9 Bastin, 1960, p. 70. Prince Paku Alam, a great-uncle of the then Sultan of Yogyakarta, was appointed in December 1814 to act as Regent during the minority of Mangku Buwono IV, who in 1816 was a boy of eleven.

RAFFLES'S MAGIC COINS

1 Raffles, 1817, vol. 2, pp. 60-61.

2 British Library, Oriental and India Office Collections, Horsfield Drawings, WD 958, f.56, pp. 319-20.

3 Raffles, 1817, vol. 2, pp. 60-61.

4 Raffles, 1817, vol. 1, p. 337.

5 Raffles, 1817, vol. 2, p. 61.

6 de Chaudoir, 1842, pl. LIII, nos 24–32.

7 Covarrubias, 1937, pp. 141–2.

8 Vecht Collection (1979), no. SA35303L.

9 Raffles, 1817, vol. 2, p. 56, plate opposite p. 57.

10 Hefner, 1985, pp. 27 and 192, figs 3–4; Scheurleer and Klokke, 1988, p. 143.

11 Hooykaas, 1973a, fig. d3; Ramseyer, 1977, p. 166, fig. 244.

12 Leeuwrik, 1982–3.

13 Ramseyer, 1977, p. 166, fig. 244.

14 Raffles, 1817, vol. 1, p. 363.

15 Raffles, 1817, vol. 1, p. 366.

16 Raffles, 1817, vol. 1, p. 355.

17 Rentse, 1936a, p. 291.

TENGGER BUDDHISM

1 Lady Raffles, 1830, p. 330.

2 Lady Raffles, 1830, p. 332.

3 Lady Raffles, 1830, p. 329.

4 Hageman, 1871, p. 6.

5 Domis, 1832.

6 Smith-Hefner, 1990, p. 290.

7 Smith-Hefner, 1990, p. 288.

8 From Hooykaas, 1974.

9 Schulte Nordholt, 1996, pp. 31-3.

WHITE ELEPHANTS AND CANNIBALS

1 Scott-Kemball, n.d., p. 10.

2 Lady Raffles, 1830, p. 181.

3 Lady Raffles, 1830, p. 181.

4 Wurtzburg, 1986, p. 360.

5 Raffles, 1929, p. 46.

6 Lady Raffles, 1830, pp. 477-8.

7 Wurtzburg, 1986, p. 562.

8 Wurtzburg, 1986, p. 716.

BIBLIOGRAPHY

ABBREVIATIONS

JMBRAS *Journal of the Malayan* [Malaysian] *Branch of the Royal Asiatic Society*, Singapore and
   Kuala Lumpur, 1923–

JSBRAS *Journal of the Straits Branch of the Royal Asiatic Society*, Singapore, 1878–1922

JSBNH *Journal of the Society for Bibliography in Natural History*

TLS *Transactions of the Linnaean Society*

Archer, M., 1962. *Natural History Drawings in the India Office Library*, London

Barley, N., 1991. *The Duke of Puddle Dock: Travels in the Footsteps of Stamford Raffles*, London

Bastin, J.S. (ed.), 1960. *The Journal of Thomas Otho Travers 1813-1820*, Singapore

Bastin, J.S., 1970. 'The first prospectus of the Zoological Society of London: new light on the
   Society's origins', *JSBNH* 5:5, pp. 369-88

Bastin, J.S., 1971. 'Raffles the Naturalist', *The Straits Times Annual for 1971*, pp. 58-63

Bastin, J.S., 1973a. 'A further note on the origins of the Zoological Society of London', *JSBNH* 6:4,
   pp. 236-41

Bastin, J.S., 1973b. 'The Java Journal of Dr Joseph Arnold', *JMBRAS* 46:1, pp. 1-92

Bastin, J.S., 1973c. 'Dr Joseph Arnold and the Discovery of *Rafflesia Arnoldi* in West Sumatra in
   1818', *JSBNH* 6:5, pp. 305-72

Bastin, J.S., 1974. 'A Further Note on Dr Joseph Arnold', *JMBRAS* 47:2, p. 149

Bastin, J.S., 1981. 'The Letters of Sir Stamford Raffles to Nathaniel Wallich 1819-1824', *JMBRAS*
   54:2, pp. 1-73

Bastin, J. S., 1990a. *The Natural History Researches of Dr Thomas Horsfield (1773-1859), First
   American Naturalist of Indonesia*, Singapore, Oxford University Press

Bastin, J.S., 1990b. 'Sir Stamford Raffles and the Study of Natural History in Penang, Singapore
   and Indonesia', *JMBRAS* 63:2, pp. 1-25

Bastin, J.S. and Moore, D.T., 1982. 'The geological researches of Dr Thomas Horsfield in
   Indonesia 1801-1819', *Bulletin of the British Museum (Natural History)*, history series 10:3,
   pp. 75-115

Bernet Kempers, A.J., 1959. *Ancient Indonesian Art*, Cambridge, Massachusetts

Blunt, W., 1976. *The Ark in the Park: The Zoo in the Nineteenth Century*, London

Boulger, D.C., 1897, repr. 1973. *The Life of Sir Stamford Raffles*, London

Brandon, J., 1966. 'Indonesia's Wayang Kulit: An enduring tradition', *Asia* 9, pp. 51-61, New York

Brayley, E.W., 1828. 'Some account of the Life and Writings, and Contributions to Science, of the late Sir Thomas Stamford Raffles, ... ', *The Zoological Journal* III, pp. 1-48, 382-400

Brooke, G.E., 1921. 'Botanic Gardens and Economic Notes', in Makepeace, W., Brooke, G.E. and Braddell, R. St (eds), *One Hundred Years of Singapore* II, pp. 63-79

Brown, R., 1821. 'An Account of a new Genus of Plants, named *Rafflesia*', *TLS* XIII, pp. 201-34

Burkill, I.H., 1916. 'William Jack's Letters to Nathaniel Wallich, 1819-1821', *JSBRAS* 73, pp. 147-208

Carey, P. (ed.), 1992. *The British in Java, 1811-1816: A Javanese account*, Oxford

Chasen, F.N., 1930. 'Raffles, the Naturalist', *Inter-Ocean* XI:3, pp. 129-31

de Chaudoir, S., 1842. *Recueil des monnaies de la Chine, du Japon, de la Corée, d'Annam et de Java*, St Petersburg

Christie, J.W., 1995. *A Preliminary Survey of Early Javanese Coinage Held in Javanese Collections*, Djakarta

Christie, J.W., 1996. 'Money and its uses in the Javanese States of the ninth to fifteenth centuries A.D.', *Journal of the Economic and Social History of the Orient* 39:3, pp. 243-86

Covarrubias, M., 1937. *Island of Bali*, New York

Crawfurd, J., 1820. *History of the Indian Archipelago*, Edinburgh

Cribb, J., 1996. 'Chinese coin finds from South India and Sri Lanka', in *Numismatic Panorama: Essays in Memory of the late Shri S.M. Shukla*, K.K. Maheshwari and B. Rath (eds), New Delhi, pp. 253-69

Cribb, J., 1999. *Magic Coins of Java, Bali and the Malay Peninsula, Thirteenth to Twentieth Centuries: A Catalogue based on the Raffles Collection of Coin-shaped Charms from Java in the British Museum*, London

Cribb, J. and Potts, D., 1996. 'Chinese coin finds from Arabia and the Arabian Gulf', *Arabian Archaeology and Epigraphy* 7, pp. 108-18

Dawson, W.R., 1958. *The Banks Letters: A Calendar of the manuscript correspondence of Sir Joseph Banks preserved in the British Museum, the British Museum (Natural History) and other collections in Great Britain*, London

Deleuze, M., 1823. *History and Description of the Royal Museum of Natural History*, Paris

Bibliography

Desmond, R., 1982. *The India Museum 1801-1879*, London

Djoemena, Nian S., 1993. 'Batik Treasures of the Special Region of Yogyakarta', in Nabholz-Kartaschoff *et al.* (eds), *Weaving Patterns of Life: Indonesian Textiles Symposium 1991*, Museum of Ethnography, Basel

Domis, H.J., 1832. 'Aantekeningen over Het Gebergte Tinger', *Verhandelingen van het Bataviaasch Gennotschap van Kunsten en Wetencshappen* 13, pp. 325-56

Farquhar, W., 1820. 'Account of a new species of Tapir found in the Peninsula of Malacca', *Asiatick Researches* XIII:xi, pp. 417-27

Forge, A., 1989. 'Batik Patterns of the Early Nineteenth Century', in Gittinger, M. (ed.), *To Speak with Cloth: Studies in Indonesian textiles*, Museum of Cultural History, University of California, Los Angeles

Geertz, C., 1960. *The Religion of Java*, London

Hageman, J., 1871. *Tengger, Gebergte en Bevolking*, Passoeroean

Hanitch, R., 1913. 'Letters of Nathaniel Wallich relating to the Establishment of Botanical Gardens in Singapore', *JSBRAS* 65, pp. 39-48

Hefner, R.W., 1985. *Hindu Javanese, Tengger Tradition and Islam*, Princeton

Hill, A.H., 1955. 'The Hikayat Abdullah: An annotated translation', *JMBRAS* 28:3, pp. 1-345

Hobart, A., 1979. Craftsmanship, Iconography and Background of the Balinese Shadow Play (doctoral thesis), London

Hobart, A., 1985. *Balinese Shadow Play Figures: Their social and ritual significance*, British Museum Occasional Paper no. 49, London

Hobart, A., 1987. *Dancing Shadows of Bali*, London

Holt, C., 1967. *Art in Indonesia: Continuities and Change*, Ithaca

Hooker, W.J., 1830. 'Description of Malayan Plants, By William Jack', *Botanical Miscellany* I, pp. 273-90

Hooker, W.J., 1831. 'Description of Malayan Plants, By William Jack', *Botanical Miscellany* II, pp. 60-89

Hooker, W.J., 1834. 'Description of Malayan Plants, By William Jack', *The Journal of Botany* I, pp. 358-80

Hooker, W.J., 1835. 'Description of Malayan Plants, By William Jack. With a brief Memoir of the Author, and Extracts from his Correspondence', *Companion to the Botanical Magazine* I, pp. 121-57, 219-24, 253-72

Hooykaas, C., 1973. *Religion of Bali*, Leiden

Hooykaas, C., 1974. *Cosmogony and Creation in Balinese Tradition*, The Hague

Hooykaas-van Leeuwen Boomkamp, J.H., 1961a. 'Ritual Purification of a Balinese Temple', *Vehandelingen der Koninklijke Nederlandse Akademie van Wetenschappen*, vol. 68, Amsterdam

Hooykaas-van Leeuwen Boomkamp, J.H., 1961b. 'The Myth of the young cowherd and the little girl', *Bijdragen Koninklijk Instituut voor Taal-, Land- en Volkenkunde*, pp. 267-78

Horsfield, T., 1821-4. *Zoological Researches in Java, and the Neighbouring Islands*, London

Horsfield, T., 1825. 'Description of the *Rimau-Dahan* of the inhabitants of Sumatra, a new species of Felis, discovered in the Forests of Bencoolen, by Sir T. Stamford Raffles, late Lieutenant Governor of Fort Marlborough, &c. &c. &c.', *Zoological Journal* I, pp. 542-54

Horsfield, T., 1838-52. *Plantæ Javanicæ' Rariores, Descriptæ Iconibusque Illustratæ, Quas in Insula Java, Annis 1802-1818, Legit et Investigavit Thomas Horsfield, M.D. ...*, Bennett, J.J. and Brown, R. (eds), London

Jardine, W., 1834. 'Memoir of Sir Thomas Stamford Raffles', *The Naturalist's Library, Ornithology* IV:2, pp. 19-66

Kant-Achilles, M., Seltmann, F. and Schumacher, R., 1990. *Wayang Beber: das wiederentdecke Bildrollen-Drama Zentral-Javas*, Stuttgart

Keeler, W., 1987. *Javanese Shadow Plays, Javanese Selves*, Princeton

Keeler, W., 1992. *Javanese Shadow Plays*, Singapore

Koentjaraningrat, 1985. *Javanese Culture*, Singapore

Lohuizen-de Leeuw, J.E. van, 1984. *Indo-Javanese Metalwork*, Stuttgart

Mabberley, D.J., 1985. *Jupiter Botanicus Robert Brown of the British Museum*, Braunschweig

Marsden, W., 1823-5. *Numismata Orientalia Illustrata*, 2 parts, London

Mauss, M., 1972. *A General Theory of Magic*, trans. R. Brian, London

Maxwell, W.G., 1908. 'Some Early Accounts of the Malay Tapir', *JSBRAS* 52, pp. 97-104

Mellema, R.L., 1954. *Wayang Puppets: Carving, Colouring and Symbolism*, trans. M. Hood, Amsterdam

Merrill, E.D., 1952. 'William Jack's Genera and Species of Malaysian Plants', *Journal of the Arnold Arboretum* XXXIII:3, pp. 199-251

Millies, H.C., 1871. *Recherches sur les monnaies des indigènes de l'archipel indien et de la péninsule malaie*, The Hague

Mitchell, P. Chalmers, 1929. *Centenary History of the Zoological Society of London*, London

Bibliography

Netscher, E. and van der Chijs, J.A., 1863. *De Munten van Nederlandsch Indië, Beschreven en Afgebeeld*, Batavia

Pigeaud, T.G.T., 1960-62. *Java in the 14th Century: A Study in Cultural History* (*The Nagara-Kertagama* by Rawaki Prapanca of Majapahit, AD 1365), Koninklijk Instituut voor Taal-, Land- en Volkenkunde (translation series) 4:4, The Hague

Raffles, Lady S., 1830. *Memoir of the Life and Public Services of Sir Thomas Stamford Raffles, FRS &c. Particularly in the Government of Java, 1811-1816, and of Bencoolen and its Dependencies 1817-1824; with Details of the Commerce and Resources of the Eastern Archipelago ...*, London

Raffles, T.S., 1817, repr. 1965, 1978. *The History of Java*, 2 vols, London; repr. Kuala Lumpur, with Introduction [1978] by Bastin, J.S., pp. v-xxi

Raffles, T.S., 1821-3. 'Descriptive Catalogue of a Zoological Collection, made on account of the Honourable East India Company, in the Island of Sumatra and its Vicinity, under the Direction of Sir Thomas Stamford Raffles, Lieutenant-Governor of Fort Marlborough; with additional Notices illustrative of the Natural History of those Countries', *TLS* XIII, pp. 239-74, 277-340

Raffles, Sir T.S., 1929. *Raffles's Report on Japan to the Secret Committee of the English East India Company*, Kobe

Ramseyer, U., 1977. *The Art and Culture of Bali*, Oxford

Rassers, W.H., 1959. *Pañji, the Culture Hero: A Structural Study of Religion in Java*, The Hague

Rentse, A., 1936a. 'The Kelantan shadow play', *JMBRAS* XIV:3, pp. 284-301

Rentse, A., 1936b. 'Majapahit amulets in Kelantan', *JMBRAS* XIV:3, pp. 302-4, pls XVI-XVII

Scherren, H., 1905. *The Zoological Society of London: A Sketch of its Foundation and Development and the Story of its Farm, Museum, Gardens, Menagerie and Library*, London

Scheurleer, P.L. and Klokke, M.J., 1988. *Ancient Indonesian Bronzes*, Leiden

Schulte Nordholt, H., 1996. *The Spell of Power: A History of Balinese Politics 1680-1940*, Leiden

Scott-Kemball, J., 1970. *Javanese Shadow Puppets*, London

Scott-Kemball, J., n.d. The Raffles Gamelan (unpublished manuscript)

Smith-Hefner, N.J., 1990. 'The Litany of "The World's Beginning": A Hindu-Javanese Purification Text', *Journal of Southeast Asian Studies* XXI:2, pp. 287-328

Steenis-Kruseman, M.J. van, 1950. 'Malaysian Plant Collectors and Collections, being a Cyclopaedia of Botanical Exploration in Malaysia ...', *Flora Malesiana*, Steenis, C.G.G.J. van (ed.), 1:1, pp. 1-639

Swainson, W., 1840. *Taxidermy; with the Biography of Zoologists, and Notices of Their Works*, London

Tambiah, S.J., 1984. *The Buddhist Saints of the Forest and the Cult of Amulets*, Cambridge

Thierry, F., 1987. *Amulettes de Chine et du Viet-nam, rites magiques et symboliques de la Chine ancienne*, Paris

Wicks, R.S., 1986. 'Monetary developments in Java between the ninth and sixteenth centuries: a numismatic perspective', *Indonesia* 42, pp. 42-77

Wicks, R.S., 1992. *Money, Markets and Trade in Early Southeast Asia: The Development of Indigenous Monetary Systems to AD 1400*, Ithaca

Wurtzburg, C.E., 1954, repr. 1986. *Raffles of the Eastern Isles*, London, Singapore